CITROËN 2CV

THE UGLY DUCKLING?

Ernst van Altena

Foulis

Haynes

A FOULIS Motoring Book

First published 1983

English language edition published 1986. Reprinted 1987 & 1988

Published by:
Haynes Publishing Group
Sparkford, Nr. Yeovil, Somerset BA22 7JJ,
England.

Haynes Publications Inc.
861 Lawrence Drive, Newbury Park,
California 91320, USA.

British Library cataloguing in publication data
   Van Altena, Ernst
   Citroën 2CV : the ugly duckling?
   1. Citroën automobile
   I. Title
   629.2'222   TL215.C56
   ISBN 0-85429-551-8

Original development and production: Jan Veldhuizen
Design: Peter Koch
Printed in England by: J.H. Haynes & Co.

This book was made possible through the collaboration of the Marketing, Publicity and External Relations Service of Citroën Nederland bv and the authorized dealers of 'Het Eerst Uur', in particular J. van Gorp, F. van der Meulen, C. den Ouden, J.D. van Steenbergen and C. Wolf (†).

In 1957, when I was 23 years old, I bought my first car, a grey 1949 Citroën *Traction Avant* 11 *normale,* for 1250 guilders. Four years later, when there were 155,000 miles on the clock, the universal packed up in the middle of the Dam square in Amsterdam. The scrap value was all of 75 guilders.

Because of back trouble I was then suffering, my doctor advised me to buy a Citroën 1D – I wish doctors always gave such sound advice! Between 1961 and 1967 I wore out three 1Ds, one light blue one, one red and one dark blue. In our century a man's life is often charted by his cars: in 1968 I drove a borrowed 2CV, then an AMI-4 and in 1969 an AMI-6. In 1970 I aspired to a then 'Car of the Year', a Citroën GS, and I am now on my sixth of the type, a GSA.

Besides this from 1978 to 1982 we had another 2CV, a yellow one, as a runabout. When in 1982 a violent hailstorm punched holes in its roof and the ignition could only be protected from incoming rain and snow with a plastic sandwich wrapper, when the braking distance at 15mph had reached 165 yards, and the front-seat passenger's legs and feet could assist acceleration or braking via the gaps in the floor, we gave our 2CV to a lady neighbour. She was able to salvage so many parts for her own venerable 2CV that she is now driving around as good as new again: only for this car does the 'old + old = brand new' formula work.

What I am trying to explain by all this is that it was not altogether illogical for Citroën of Holland and the original Dutch publishers of this book to have sought me out to write a small volume on the 2CV. Whilst I earn a not inconsiderable part of my daily bread by translating French plays, books and poetry, at heart I am a Citroën fanatic.

I consider it right and proper that the 2CV, the 'Ugly Duckling', should be honoured with a special book in its fourth decade of life: a knighthood as it were! For this car, ingeniously conceived in the crisis year of the 1930s, has managed to persist through all the intervening fashions: it is a part of French culture – more, it *is* French culture ... on wheels. Rather nonchalant, with a Basque beret on its head, and 'if we can't manage it today never mind, tomorrow we will' kind of attitude, a lot of noise and commotion about nothing much, regularly late, very conservative (as even left-wing Frenchmen are), chauvinistic, but on the other hand hospitable, open-hearted, funfilled, practical, individualistic and freedom loving.

In 1948 the 2CV was a French revolution in motoring. It was threatened with execution at the hands of the expert critics, but spread its influence all over Europe under the watchwords of *Liberté, Egalité, Fraternité.* That the 2CV became so very popular in Holland in particular, where it acquired its honoured 'Ugly Duckling' nickname, is without doubt due to Voltaire, who called Holland a land of *canaux, canards, canaille:* which might now be freely rendered as 'a country where scoundrels bump along beside the canals in 2CVs'.

I wish you all as much pleasure in reading this book as I had in writing it.

Ernst van Altena
Landsmeer, Holland

The Great Mistake

It was 1936 and the end of the world depression was by no means in sight. France itself, was bowed under economic gloom; there was bitter poverty and much social distress. In their struggle simply to exist, people living on the poverty line could not even think of cars: a car was the symbol of the privileged classes. And that is how cars were designed: gleaming status symbols for the happy few, for the world of Scott Fitzgerald and his Zelda, for arrogant men of state and obsequious doctors. The age of the Ford Model T – the car for everyman – was over. The designer dictated the motoring fashions of those days: cars had to be big, heavy, low and swish.

André Citroën, the brilliant designer of Dutch extraction (his father had added the two dots to the name when he went to France; in Dutch the name means 'lemon', as it does in a number of languages in its various spellings), had had to give up the unequal struggle with these dictators of automobile fashion some years before. In order to resist the great might of the American car industry as the depression began he had had to attract foreign capital. As part of the financial deal, the bankers imposed a business director on him and with that, conflict was on the agenda. The self-willed Citroën, who had once put his name up in house-high illuminated letters on the Eiffel tower, had always made his own decisions and refused to listen to a money man who knew nothing about cars. Before very long he had sent the financial director packing and, therefore, the foreign capital as well. He wanted to produce *real* cars, not transient commercial packages. With this policy, however, he brought about his own ruin. His company went bankrupt and not long after, in 1935, he died a disappointed man. As a result, the direction of the firm had to be left in other hands – happily in those of others who wanted to go on working in his way; men concerned with the character of a car, not its fancy wrapping.

Citroën was taken over by the Michelin Tyre Company. Tyre manufacturers have a hard-headed outlook and want to see as many tyres as possible worn out. One car takes five tyres and you earn much less on five tyres than on one car; and the more exclusive the cars, the less chance the tyre industry has of maintaining its existence. On purely economic grounds ancillary supply companies have a great interest in the wider distribution – the 'socialization' – of the car, and in the ready-made rather than the bespoke automobile.

Michelin put two directors in charge of Citroën. One was Pierre Michelin, and the other Pierre Boulanger who can be regarded as the father of the Ugly Duckling.

Left-hand page: Prototype of the 2CV.

André Citroën (1878 – 1935).

Boulanger was a remarkable man. He was born in northern France in 1885 and had to earn his own living at an early age. On his 23rd birthday, after completing his military service, he departed for the United States. After holding down twelve jobs without incident which included working on a ranch and as a tram driver before becoming an architectural draughtsman in Seattle, he left America and set up his own building company in Canada.

When the First World War broke out he returned to France, where he served in the French air force for four years, mainly engaged in aerial photography of enemy positions, attaining the rank of Captain. Subsequently, through his friendship with one of the Michelin sons, he went to work for that firm at Clermont-Ferrand where he was given the task of building housing for the Michelin workers.

Aviation and low-cost housing do not immediately come to mind as ideal starting points for a career in the car industry, but we shall see how it was these very elements that played an important part in the realization of the 2CV project.

Above: Prototype with one headlamp, a hand-operated windscreen wiper and a starting handle.

Right: Air force captain and reconnaissance plane pilot Pierre Boulanger in 1917 (left of photo).

Far right: Pierre Boulanger in about 1939 – 'father of the 2CV'.

At Epinal in France they do a lot of printing of coloured illustrations for children's books – but the following was no fairy tale. In 1967 a 41-year-old inhabitant climbed on to his roof to adjust the TV aerial. The tiles were icy and he slipped and fell 30 feet on to a 2CV parked below in front of the house. His weight carried him through its roof but, thanks to the protective compliance of the suspension, he landed unharmed on the back seat.

Two farmers in clogs

After spending 1935 restoring order to Citroën affairs, Boulanger went to its design office at the beginning of 1936 with a remarkable commission. He told the office that it should begin research into the feasibility of building a small car that could 'carry two farmers in clogs, 50 kilos [110 lb] of potatoes or a small barrel at a maximum speed of 50 km/h [30 mph] with a petrol consumption of 1 lit/33 km (90 mpg)'.

Boulanger also made it clear that the car would have to be able to carry passengers in the maximum comfort on the poorest roads, that an inexperienced farmer's wife should be able to drive it, that it should cost no more than one-third of the price of the famous Citroën II *Traction Avant,* and that it mattered not one bit what the car looked like.

Although the Citroën design staff began to think that Boulanger was not altogether right in

the head, the idea was given serious thought. The strong agricultural emphasis derived from Boulanger's own observation of the farmers in the villages around Clermont-Ferrand. They left home very early every morning to take their produce by horse and cart to market in town, where their wives and children sold it while the farmers waited in the *bistros* until they could drive home again in the afternoon. France had a great deal of countryside with many small peasant farmers: if car ownership could be made feasible for them, a fantastic and, as yet untapped, market would be opened up. If the farmer's wife were able to drive the car herself, her husband would be able to stay on the farm and use dozens of extra working hours to increase his production.

The talented designer André Lefebvre, a man with the *Traction Avant* already to his

2CV prototype as discovered after the Second World War serving as a tyre-testing vehicle for Michelin.

Don't cram people into a car, but build the car around people – Boulanger's starting point.

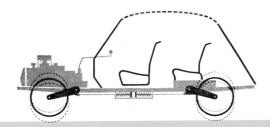

credit, was entrusted with working out this 'ridiculous' concept. The project was given the code name TPV *(Toute Petite Voiture:* 'very small car'), and before a line appeared on a drawing board, extensive research was carried out. In five months about 10,000 members of the travelling public were asked their ideas on owning a car. Modern market research in 1936! The result confirmed that Boulanger was right to a remarkable degree. Not only French farmers but a much bigger segment of the *petit-bourgeoisie* were interested in the possibility of having a car.

With this result of research to hand Lefebvre was able to get to work. His chief aim was to keep the weight of the car below 660lb. He planned to achieve this by not having a chassis, by reinforcing the bodywork with bracing wires, and by making it of aluminium. On these two latter points, derived from

contemporary aviation practice, there was a meeting of minds between Boulanger, the former wartime flier, and Lefebvre, the ex-aircraft builder. It was true that aluminium was still a very expensive material but the expectation was that it would soon become cheaper – one of Boulanger's few miscalculations. Corrugated aluminium sheeting would be used for the car body, as on the contemporary German Junkers aircraft; corrugations were a characteristic feature of the bonnet of the later 2CV for quite a time.

Handlebars and lengths of fabric

At the beginning of 1937 Lefebvre presented his first prototype – the 'softest' car in the world. Everything was made of aluminium except the four suspension arms, which were of magnesium. The gearbox had no reverse; torsion springs under the back seat took care of the suspension; instead of an electric starter there was a crank handle; the front seats were lengths of fabric hung from the roof; the roof was simply a cover stretched over an aluminium frame; the steering acted like bicycle handlebars directly on the wheels; the car threatened to topple over at every bend; the windows were of cellulose acetate (Perspex); the doors were semi-circular (this was derived from the 'Bauhaus circle', which revealed the hand of the architect Boulanger, and remained a characteristic of the 2CV); the engine came from a 300 cc BMW motorcycle. And most important of all: after riding in it for some 50 yards Lefebvre decided to take the whole thing to pieces and start again. One prototype after another now followed, but without any great success. One of these prototypes caught fire near Champigny. A short-circuit ignited the petrol tank, and there was a blinding flash when the flames reached the magnesium suspension arms, demonstrating clearly why photographers used magnesium powder for their flash guns. An electricity supply cable 30 feet above the flaming wreck was burned through. In the end only the carburettor, which was not made of aluminium, was left.

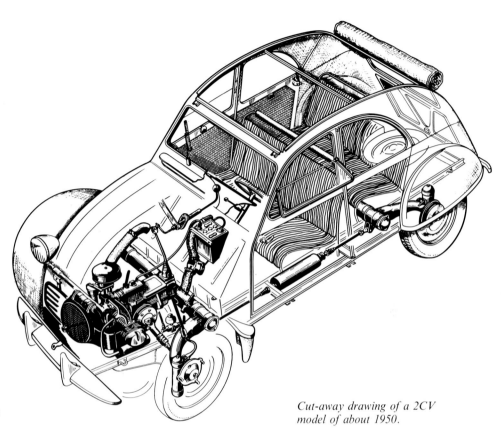

Cut-away drawing of a 2CV model of about 1950.

Aluminium prototype as ready for production in 1939, but dismantled after the German invasion of France.

For the African farmer too: three wives, two goats, the harvest and the man himself.

Magnesium suspension arms. They burned like flares.

In the meantime the worn-out BMW 300 cc engine was replaced by a specially built water-cooled unit of 375 cc. The attempt to stay under 660 lb was given up. The springs remained a great problem, and the vehicle was too 'soft' and juddered whenever the brake pedal was touched.

More and more sceptics were to be found among the old hands at Citroën. They considered that much too much time was being wasted on the unsightly and unlikely contraption, and in the strictest secrecy they hatched a revolutionary plot. They designed a mini version of the Citroën II *Traction Avant*, but when Boulanger eventually found out what was going on there was a swift end to the conspiracy.

In 1937 completion of the TPV project became really urgent. After Pierre Michelin died in a car accident part of the management of the tyre company fell on Boulanger's shoulders. As a result he saw even more clearly how important it was to open up the car market to the masses; at the same time he feared that the competition would get there before him, for Citroën's experiments had not remained a secret to its rivals.

Into hiding in the grounds of a former palace

To prevent industrial espionage the 2CV had to go into hiding. An enclosed park was bought, in which the summer palace of Louis Philippe, the Citizen King, had once stood, at La Ferté-Vidame in the Eure-et-Loire district. In an area of 1980 acres the first test track of 1¹/₂ miles was laid out. The park was heavily guarded and only a very small team of TPV stalwarts was allowed entry. The test drivers doing their daily rounds startled many a hare or rabbit, for the local population, accustomed formerly to poaching in the grounds, was strictly excluded. The test drivers sat on canvas seats on an open platform without any form of bodywork and wore thick flying overalls, for the testing went on summer and winter.

In 1938, when some 20 prototypes had been tested, Lefebvre made a basic alteration to his concept. The whole vehicle was no longer to be supported on the four swinging arms but would be carried on an aluminium floorpan. The problem with this was that the bodywork had to be welded to this plate at a number of points, and aluminium welding was still at an experimental stage.

Despite all this Pierre Boulanger planned to put the car on the market in 1939 and he

with its riding qualities, not with the practicality of the vehicle for a non-expert public that could not afford high maintenance costs. And in this area the design fell short on a number of points. A layman could not drain the radiator of the water-cooled engine himself; he could not change the oil unless he had an inspection pit or a car lift; he could hardly even top up the oil himself, for to reach the cap he would have to

Photographing the 2CV was not allowed. Clandestine snap of the TPV on the test track at La Ferté-Vidame, about 1942.

Citroën statement: flat floorpan, right on the propeller shaft, front-wheel drive!

informed Michelin at Clermont-Ferrand that he was proposing the following production plan: May 1939, 10 – 15 per day; June, 100 per day; July, 250 per day. Then in December 1938 technical reports threw a spanner in the works. The latest prototype might appear roadworthy to the test drivers, but they were only concerned

unscrew five bolts and remove the whole front left-hand wing. To check the oil level in the gearbox he would have to unscrew the five bolts on the front right-hand wing, then take out the battery in order to reach the gearbox. Refilling the gearbox with oil could only be done in an inspection pit or on a lift.

To mark the wedding of the Prince of Wales and Lady Diana the Citroën agent for Kent obtained the Lord Chamberlain's permission to sell a Dyane dedicated to the royal bride. The bodywork was in red, white and blue, the wheels were gilded, there was a coat of arms on each front door, and the wedding date and the name 'Dyana' appeared on the boot lid. A 2CV by appointment.

Left-hand page, above: Salon d'Automobile, Paris 1948. For the first time in 14 years Citroën was presenting a new model. Everything about it was new. The unveiling took place in the presence of Vincent Auriol, President of the French Republic. Press and public reaction ranged from amazed to thunderstruck. Was it a car or a great mistake!

At a height of 4000 m (13,000 ft) on the borders of India and Tibet lies the little state, formerly a monarchy, of Sikkim. In 1958 the maharajah of this postage stamp country provided himself with a 2CV as his state car. He chose it because more regal limousines baulked at Sikkim's precipitous cart tracks.

Left-hand page, below: Frenchman Jacques Pochon-Davignon worked in Indochina from 1945 to 1968, and then it was time for him and the other five members of his family to return home. However, he wanted to see something of the world on the way back so he treated his wife and children to a 24,000 mile, eight-month ride in the 2CV delivery van. From Laos they drove to Benares via Bangkok, Singapore, Madras, Ceylon (Sri Lanka), Mysore and Hyderabad. Surfaced roads were few and far between on that stage. From Benares they travelled on through Teheran, Bagdad, Jerusalem, Beirut, Istanbul, Athens, Belgrade, Milan, Geneva, Munich, Stuttgart, Brussels and so on to Paris. Quite a repatriation!

The 2CV naturally competed in the Caltex Economy Test drive of 1959. The course went from Freudenstadt in Germany through France, Luxemburg, Belgium, the Netherlands and on to Copenhagen. The 1240 mile journey took in snow-covered mountain roads as well as urban stages. After five days the 2CV emerged as the thriftiest car by far, with 75 mpg consumption.

In 1958-9 Jacques Seguele and J.C. Brandt of Perpignan undertook a round-the-world journey in a 2CV. After 15,500 miles they were crossing the Atacama Desert in Chile when their crankcase cap shook loose and all the oil drained away; this was disastrous, as they had no spare oil left. Then a solitary Indian appeared, took stock of the situation and pulled a bunch of bananas out of his bag. He peeled them and then stuffed them into the crankcase. With this fruity lubrication the 2CV completed the remaining 185 miles across the desert without damage and (replenished with rear oil) arrived back in France after a further 46,000 miles.

And that was by no means all: the carburettor, too, was accessible only after wholesale dismantling, and there was nowhere really suitable for stowing a jack. Measuring petrol quantity was nearly impossible; the fuel feed was at such an angle that the dipstick gave a distorted reading, and the spout on the petrol tank was of such soft material that a clumsy pump attendant could split or bend it so that the top no longer fitted. The rear view was inadequate for anyone over 5 ft 5 in, whose eyes would be level with the inside of the hood, not the rear window. The Perspex pane was so laden with static that it attracted dust and turned, in effect, into frosted glass, and no one had thought of fitting a rear-view mirror. The steering wheel was so low that the driver's knees were always in the way; and if he was on the tall side his right knee jammed under the gear lever. The handbrake hardly worked. And on every bend the car either 'sailed close to the wind' or leaned over on one ear, etc. etc.

The reports contained positive points, too, but these mainly concerned the mechanical qualities of the car tested during the many trial runs. The test drivers had had no chance at all of (and probably little interest in) including the comfort of driver and passengers in their trials. The windscreen proved not to be watertight. The canvas of the seats was so stiff and rough that you could not slide in or out of the car; and a person of any size at all could not get into the driver's seat. The left-hand doors (offside in Continental terms) had no handles on the outside, not even on the driver's side where it was really necessary and, according to the reports, the inside handles broke off very quickly in use. Draughts came in all round the doors and two people were needed to put up the canvas hood. The ventilation arrangement would not shut and whistled when the car was in motion and the heating was quite inadequate for winter. In short, the TPV was far from being ready for use by the public – and, it should be added, many of these observations will be familiar to early 2CV drivers of the 1950s and 60s.

There was further tinkering with the prototype. The car proved so light that any load in the back – readers will remember the farmer with his 50 kilos of potatoes or his cask of wine – made its nose point heavenward; and overloading there caused the bodywork to scrape along the road in a shower of sparks. The vehicle still juddered at the slightest application of the brakes. New ideas were put forward to counter all these faults; they were ingenious but had the drawback of making the TPV steadily heavier and thirstier – which was hardly the original intention.

Glow-worms and fishbones

Boulanger's obsession with keeping the 2CV light led jokers at Citroën to make such suggestions as, 'Let's replace the headlamps with glow-worms – they don't weigh anything and don't tax the battery'; or 'Put in rotting fishbones as rearlights – they fluoresce in the dark'.

In 1938, however, Boulanger did order a trial production series of 250 TPVs for 1939. For the factory workers this order proved a minor disaster. None of them was familiar with working in aluminium and the welding machines developed by AEG that should have come from Germany did not arrive – because of the threat of war. This meant the welders had to tackle the new material with the standard steel-welding electrodes. Often they burned holes in the material and even began to show symptoms of skin infections. Everything had to be done by hand, and any honest calculation showed that the low costs ideal was going by the board.

Then, on 2 September 1939, the first complete TPV was rolled out of the factory doors. Following her non-aggression pact with Stalin, Germany invaded Poland, and France and Britain declared war on Germany. France mobilized, production of the TPV was stopped immediately and the only completed prototype 2CV was to remain the solitary production example for the time being. That one TPV soon disappeared from sight. According to the story, a mechanic drove off in it unnoticed to Niort to pick up a consignment from the Citroën parts store there. He had engine trouble on the way, however, and the car was subsequently discovered, in 1942, in a Citroën garage on the main road to Orléans. No one had missed it for all that time.

The German army occupied Paris, and Citroën was given a *Verwalter*, or administrator, who was a former DKW director. Pierre Boulanger feared that he would be compelled to produce his TPVs for the Germany army – they would make excellent cross-country vehicles. Boulanger was probably wrong here; the Germans had their own *Kraft durch Freude* ('Strength through Joy') car, the Volkswagen, which had reached a much more practical stage of development and, typically, was a much sounder and more solid job than the French effort. But Boulanger, the First World War flier, was understandably very anti-German and sabotaged production of all Citroën models, especially the trucks the occupiers needed so badly.

Destroying the evidence

In his anxiety to prevent any items connected with the TPV falling into German hands Boulanger ordered the destruction of all prototypes, at whatever stage, as well as all drawings and calculations. For once his word was not entirely law. Several old hands, who had put a lot into the TPV, had one example of the prototype, which was to have been shown at the 1939 Paris Salon, stowed away in various crates. It did not emerge from its hiding places until 1970 and, when reassembled, it worked right away. The only aluminium TPV from 1939 had no trafficators. The lower part of the side windows opened upwards to allow the driver to give hand signals. It had only one headlamp, as French regulations did not actually prescribe two. It had a starting handle, not an electric self-starter. The front seats were still suspended deckchair-fashion from the roof. The doors were opened from the inside by cords. And the top speed produced by the water-cooled, three-gear creation was barely 44 mph.

Quite unintentionally a second prototype from a much earlier series was preserved. This miniature lorry was apparently in service after

Opposite: Front and rear of the 1939 prototype.

'Bauhaus-style' circle and deckchair type seats supported from the roof: the interior of the original 2CV.

the war at Michelin in Clermont-Ferrand as a test vehicle for tyres. Enforced idleness during the war years gave Boulanger the idea of totally revising his plans for the TPV. Great though his love for his baby was, now that he had been able to stand back from it, he realized that it could not be a commercial success in its pre-war form. Aluminium and magnesium, however little maintenance they needed, required too much initial outlay so that the retail price of the car would have been too high. They were also difficult materials to work with, and therefore expensive in wages terms, this, too, pushing up the price. He had new costings carried out and these showed that the TPV would be at least 40 per cent more expensive than the market would bear. A new specification was therefore drawn up, in which the aluminium was replaced by flat or slightly curved steel plate, with steel tubes to give the necessary rigidity. Boulanger was not happy about this – he felt that durability, and therefore low maintenance costs, had to be taken into consideration when setting the purchase price of a car. In the end, however, he could only accept the reality of the situation. Returning to his starting point – that the TPV should above all be a useful vehicle for farmers – he initiated research into how far it was possible for the engine to be used to drive all

kinds of agricultural machinery. Even a secret project for a TPV tractor appeared on the drawing boards. There was also research into replacing the starting handle by a device, placed under the dashboard, of the type used on an outboard motor: a flywheel about which is wound a pull cord. It was discarded, however, when Boulanger injured his own hand on the prototype of this gadget.

These plans, clandestine in the sense of not being known to the *Verwalter,* remained paper projects for the time being for, even if there had been the freedom to carry them out, the necessary materials were in increasingly short supply. Tyres, for example, were soon simply not to be had. A plan to develop specially massive tyres for the TPV (to try and prevent the possibility of a blow-out) remained in the realms of theory, fortunately for later 2CV drivers.

Another picture of the 1948 Salon d'Automobile where 1,300,000 visitors were confronted with the 2CV for the first time. The sarcasm of the motoring correspondents knew no bounds. One American critic asked if Citroën 'included a can opener with it'.

No more anti-freeze

In 1941 the gifted auto engineer Walter Becchia left Talbot for Citroën; he was followed in 1943 by Talbot's carburettor specialist Lucien Girard. Both had had difficulties at Talbot with the German occupiers. This pair were Europe's greatest experts, with the benefit of vast experience. Becchia was not happy with the 375 cc engine that was still used for the prototype TPV. It was sluggish and produced too little power, and starting it in temperatures below 5° C (41° F) appeared impossible. There was also the problem of the anti-freeze in the small radiator, which had to be changed too often.

In 1944 Becchia suggested to Boulanger that the problems should be solved by designing a completely new air-cooled engine. Within a week the engine was there on paper and materials for building a trial model were assembled with great difficulty from here and there. Within a few weeks the power unit was being run at full speed on a test bench: full speed because Becchia realized that future 2CV drivers would always go flat out.

The test model ran continuously for 500 hours and behaved splendidly. When Boulanger came to have a look at it, however, he reacted with fury; the gearbox had four gears and he was implacably opposed to this. His original concept was for a maximum of three gears, proceeding on the basis that the 'unskilled farmer's wife' would find three quite difficult enough to manage. Becchia waited until Boulanger's anger had subsided then calmly pointed out that there were only three *gears:* the fourth was the overdrive. Boulanger accepted this explanation – which, incidentally is why on the first 2CVs the plate was marked with the figures 1-2-3 and the letter S (for *surmultipliée,* 'overdrive').

We may laugh now, but subsequent practice showed that Boulanger was not altogether wrong in his estimation of the capabilities of some less skilled drivers. Veterans from the Citroën garages still tell some marvellous stories about drivers who found all that business with changing gears far too complicated and drove around all day in first. From my own experience I know of a 2CV driver who changes from first through second and up to third at the beginning of every drive, then stays put in third no matter what the speed – but grumbles when the car judders on bends or uphill. *He* never uses the overdrive.

France was liberated in 1944 and Boulanger was itching to make a real start with TPV production. However, the prototype was far from ready for production. It was true that aluminium and magnesium had been dropped, so that problems of welding techniques and costs in that area had been overcome, and there was now a good engine available, but many other difficulties were a long way from solution and the roadholding was still abominable. A substitute for the original, much too expensive, suspension was found in compressible coil springs, enclosed in boxes and placed lengthways between the front and rear wheels. The car continued to 'shimmy', however, and lack of shock absorbers made the wheels bounce on the road. Boulanger would not hear of shock absorbers – they reminded him too much of the sleek luxury cars of top people and did not fit in with his outlook. A young engineer, answering to the 'rival' name of Léon Renault, was given the task of improving the wheel suspension to the point where the roadholding problems would vanish. He devised what he called *batteurs* (literally 'beaters', 'threshers'), which were, of course, shock absorbers, but had a change of name in an attempt to bamboozle Boulanger. Each consisted of a spring-loaded weight that worked through the law of inertia to 'damp down' the wheels. Boulanger was not deceived for long and forbade the *batteurs* once he had seen them on the test bench. Léon Renault resigned in anger but was brought back six months later – as were the *batteurs,* despite the objection that they added 44 lb to the total weight of the car.

Heavier and heavier

The car's weight remained a great problem. As the vehicle matured its weight increased. The test model exceeded 880 lb, which Boulanger simply would not accept. He had the car taken to pieces and personally weighed each part, asking his collaborators whether there was anything left that could be made smaller, lighter or thinner. In despair one of the engineers even suggested using hollow bolts, as this would make a difference of half a gram per bolt. A totally 'stripped-down' version was built in which even the accelerator pedal was replaced by a hand control, operated by a nylon thread. But Boulanger realized that light weight and solidity are often incompatible; he yielded and the weight went above the 880 lb mark.

In 1974 on Dutch TV there was an attempt to set up a record for the number of persons you could 'squeeze into a Citroën' [a play on the original meaning of this Dutch name]. Eighteen boys over 14 years of age were crammed into the vehicle and the doors shut on them – happily they were all able to extricate themselves.

The weight went on increasing. The Perspex windows, which attracted dust and never closed properly, had to be replaced by glass and this cost a further 11 lb. It became apparent that, all through these years of tests, the designers had been thinking too much in terms of southern France: heating had been forgotten. This oversight was rectified – adding further to the weight. Then one night during a secret trial run out on the road one of the test drivers was nearly killed by an oncoming vehicle which took the left-hand side of the car right off. Seeing the one headlamp, the approaching driver had thought it belonged to a motorcycle

The Italian designer Fulminio Bertoni, who gave the Traction Avant *and the DS19 their shapes, addressed himself to the styling of the 2CV in 1945. None of his designs, however found favour in Boulanger's eyes.*

and had not made allowances. The second headlamp was added, which again increased the weight.

The car still had no self-starter. Someone came up with the ingenious idea of making one out of a piece of elastic that you could twist and then release, more or less as on a rubber-band powered model aircraft. This did not work, however, and Boulanger continued to prefer a starting handle out in front. He even had his daughter demonstrate that a starting handle presented no problems for a woman. He was lucky – she did indeed get the car to start. The whole of 1945 was taken up with hundreds, thousands even, of test runs round the circuit at La Ferté-Vidame. Boulanger conducted the operations like a general in the field, and this personal involvement by Boulanger can be traced in the classic characteristics of the later 2CV. In contrast to the average Frenchman, for example, Boulanger was tall. He tested the seating, front and back, himself and so the 2CV was given much more leg room than comparable small cars. The same applied to the height of the hood. This had to be adapted to the boss's height and – he demanded – when he was wearing his hat!

On Sundays Boulanger used to go for a drive with his wife and for this he always used a new prototype, the petrol consumption of which he would check. The tank would be filled in front of his house in the Avenue Henri-Martin; this was done with the precision of a chemist, with the same amount measured to the last cubic centimetre. Then he would drive over exactly the same course with the same passengers in the back seat to keep the weight consistent, at a speed of 37 mph, i.e. with his foot hard down. If the consumption went above 55 mpg the prototype was returned to the engineers with a negative report.

In 1946 Boulanger became convinced that the postwar buyer would not be content with 37 mph. Auto engineer Becchia tried to persuade him that the top speed should be raised to at least 65 mph, but for Boulanger exceeding the 62 mph limit was going too far. For the time being a compromise was reached: a top speed of 56/59 mph would be attainable, but with a 62 mph potential built in.

The actual introduction year of the 2CV, 1948, had now arrived. In the automotive and technical sense the baby was ready, but aesthetically it was still lacking in every way. All the prototypes used for testing had had bodywork more or less cobbled together, based on the 1939 aluminium model it is true, but without any further styling or refinement. Body designer Bertoni sat down at the drawing board and came up with a canary-yellow car with fashionable lines. Boulanger rejected it outright. The definitive shape came from Steck and Caneau who presented their version in February 1948. It was based on practical rather than aesthetic principles, and much thought had been given to both the users' needs and the manufacturing process. Many of the 1939 features were maintained, such as the 'Bauhaus-style' circular doors. The design was approved and was due to be shown to the public for the first time at the Paris Salon in October 1948.

A few days before the doors of the Salon were opened the prototype apparently was subject to bad starting problems. In the end Boulanger had to forego his preference for an old-fashioned handle and, with a sigh, ordered the design of an electric starter. Two days later the device had been fitted – his collaborators had got one ready long before in secret.

This is how a press photographer took his illicit picture of the original TPV on the test track.

Does it exist?

After the prototype had been shown to Citroën sales staff for the first time at the end of September 1948 (they were very negative in their reactions: they thought the car was too ugly to sell), something of the heavily guarded secret began to leak to the press. The motor journalists did not really believe that the TPV would appear at the Salon: if this had been at all likely they would surely have known! So little had actually leaked out that the motoring press went on stubbornly referring to 'the so-called Citroën 3CV'. Many rumours were going the rounds. The speculation was that Citroën would be mad to put such a cheap car on the market to compete with its own *Traction Avant*, which sold so well. It was even suggested that the French government was stopping the launch of the '3CV' so that it would not cause problems for the nationalized Renault concern.

On the eve of the Salon opening the newspaper *La Presse* carried a photo of the '3CV'. By means of a ladder placed on top of his car a press photographer had managed to take a picture of a prototype on the test track. It was front-page news: the car did exist.

This clinched the matter for Boulanger: the 2CV, as it was now officially called, would be seen at the Paris Salon. And so it was – but the bonnet remained sealed. Press and public literally flung themselves on the new car. They expressed their surprise at the soft suspension: they exclaimed in chorus at its ugliness; laughed at the dipstick – but could not get over their amazement that Citroën had managed to built a

complete four-door, four-seater car with a 375 cc engine at a price around that of 'covered-in motorbikes' of the Messerschmitt type.

Production did not get under way until the following year and the 2CV became available from September 1949. Interest in the car was so great that waiting lists had to be drawn up – with strict instructions from Boulanger, who was still adhering to his original principles, that priority should be given to 'those who have to travel by car because of their work and for whom ordinary cars are too dear to buy,

And the result: front-page news throughout France – the Ugly Duckling had hatched.

The bonnet was raised at the 1949 Salon d'Automobile. Here Pierre Boulanger gives Pierre Lacoste and Antoine Pinay, French government ministers at that time, a lesson.

Blessed 2CV ...

maintain and use'. The car salesmen were only allowed to make provisional contracts, after which special Citroën inspectors visited the would-be buyers to check that they fulfilled the social criteria. Each buyer promised to report in writing on his experiences with the 2CV. One of the first customers was the French actor Daniel Ivernel, who immediately went on a non-stop drive in one to Rome, where the Italians fell about laughing when they saw the latest product of the French car industry.

The public grew more and more enthusiastic, but the motoring journalists much less so. They called the 2CV 'Citroën's great mistake', and said that it would soon go out of fashion, that a short life would be its fate, etc., etc.

A name from Hans Christian Andersen

In 1949 the first 2CV appeared on the roads of Holland. It was there that it was dubbed the

Ugly Duckling, by a Dutch journalist who knew his Andersen; it is now known by this name even in South America. Strangely enough the English – and odder still, the French – have not adopted this nor any other nickname for this much adored car.

In the 38 years of the 2CV's existence there have, of course, been some changes. Becchia, the designer of the engine, was right when he believed that the public would eventually become dissatisfied with a top speed of 37 mph. The 1950 2CV had a maximum speed of only 34 mph; the 1954 model did 47 mph; in 1961 that had been increased to 53 mph; after this the Dyane was introduced and the 62 mph limit was passed. Over the years the 2CV also became rather less spartan. In 1949 the windscreen wiper had to be worked by hand; later it was driven off the milometer – no movement, no action. In 1962 electric wipers were introduced. Then the petrol dipstick was replaced by a real fuel gauge and a speedometer and milometer were fitted.

In 1951 the 2CV delivery van appeared – another of those remarkable phenomena of which Citroën seems to have a monopoly – which became popular not only with commercial firms but also with private 'nonconformists', who made a camper of it.

The Great Mistake

A total of some 3.5 million 'great mistakes' has been manufactured. Countless numbers of them have gone to Holland where the 2CV has always been immensely popular. Here are some figures by way of comparison: in 1981, 5815 of them were sold in the Netherlands, a total only exceeded by West Germany (13,369) and Italy (6665). This means that relative to population, Holland comes top for 2CV users. Only the English speaking world rejected the car, attempts to market in Britain in 1953 and the USA in 1958 failing dismally. Not until the energy crisis of the early '70's did Citroën succeed in opening the UK market.

In 1936 Boulanger was aiming at a motoring revolution – which the 2CV has certainly brought about. Recent sociological research in France has shown that the car is still found mainly among the sections of the population for whom it was designed: for every 100 sold 21 go to the lower middle class; 18 to clerks, shop assistants etc.; 14 to manual workers; 7 to housewives; 15 to pensioners; and 6 to students.

For many years the Wegenwacht *(the Dutch AA) used 2CV vans exclusively.*

GUY-TETEAU-73

GUY-TETEAU-73

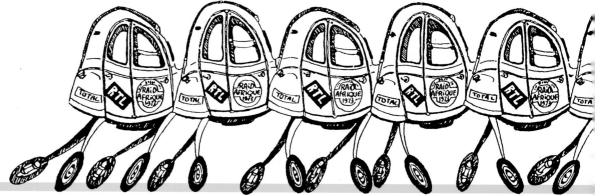

The Comic 2CV

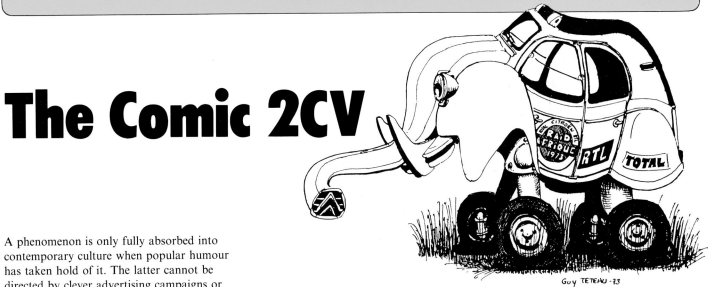

A phenomenon is only fully absorbed into contemporary culture when popular humour has taken hold of it. The latter cannot be directed by clever advertising campaigns or psychological manipulation. In the everyday language of ordinary people a spade is called a spade – or else ignored entirely. Amsterdammers will call a church a coal bucket if that is what the structure on top reminds them of, no matter how elegant the official architectural description may be. When staff reductions by the Amsterdam transport authority led to the first one-man trams, and a red stripe on the front indicated that passengers should board the vehicle at that end and buy a ticket from the driver, a newspaper offered a prize for the best name for these labour-saving conveyances. Hundreds of names were sent in and, to the regret of the transport authority, the first prize went to *Dievenwagen (dieven* means 'thieves'), it was so easy to ride in them without paying. The populace was not in the least influenced by the result and christened the new trams 'Nosebleeders'. A block of flats with rectangles of primary colours on its front was dubbed 'The Paintbox', and a yellow blob in the road to separate the traffic was called a 'jellyfish'.

A small car that waddled and was ugly by conventional fashionable standards was dubbed an 'Ugly Duckling' – which in Dutch became 'Ugly Duck', or just 'Duck'. The name may

have been launched in the press by a motoring correspondent, but it is probable that he had a good ear for the vernacular and used it. And this popular nickname has become an honourable one, applied to the 2CV even in South America – so Holland is still in the export business.

The name rapidly became current, as is shown by the following true story from about 1954, when the car could not manage more than 47 mph. A truck with a trailer was travelling at 43 mph in the right-hand lane of a four-lane motorway. A 2CV, profiting from the rig's slipstream, came alongside. The truck driver saw this and began to 'tease' the 2CV by gradually raising his speed to 45 mph. The little car was thus doomed to stay alongside the truck: it could not overtake, and the queue behind made it impossible for it to drop back. They drove abreast for some miles, like the mouse and the elephant crossing the bridge in the story ('We're making the bridge shake, aren't we!' said the mouse), until suddenly the side window on the truck opened and the driver's brawny arm appeared with a fistful of breadcrumbs which he began to sprinkle on the road in front of the Ugly Duckling.

2CVs drawn by cartoonist Guy Teteau in the guise of hippo, giraffe, camel (or dromedary) and elephant.

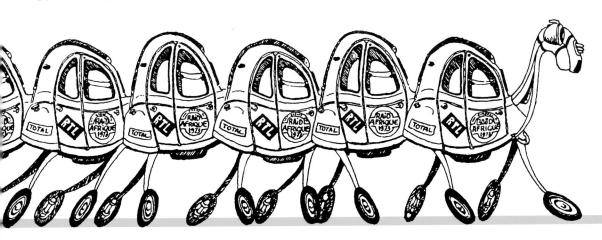

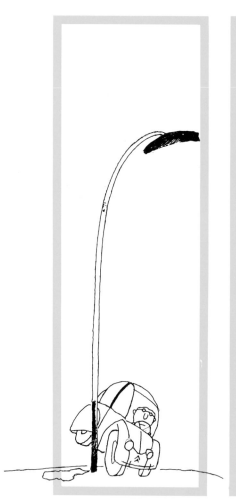

2CV collection by graphic
artist Avoine ...

avoine

The Comic 2CV

Did you hear the one about ...?

After a nickname, the next stage on the road to super-popularity is when the item starts appearing in pub stories – which is what happened to the 2CV.

A heavy truck was stopped halfway up a steep hill. A 2CV stopped alongside and the driver asked what the trouble was. 'My engine has packed up,' replied the truck driver. 'I'll give you a hand,' said the 2CV man. 'If you've got a towrope I'll pull you to the top.' Amazed, the truck driver watched as the other man fastened the towrope in place and slowly but surely hauled the juggernaut to the top of the hill. Arrived there the truck driver expressed his thanks, and his astonishment at the power of the little 2CV. 'But there's quite a lot of smoke coming from it,' he said. The 2CV driver looked at his car, scratched his head for a moment and then said, 'Oh my! I forgot to take the handbrake off!'.

Back in the 1930s Boulanger was already striving to extend car ownership. How far he was successful in this 'socializing' process is shown by the following story, which also emphasizes the 2CV's legendary suspension. Two boys were walking through a wood when they spotted a 2CV parked among the bushes. The car was giving a vigorous demonstration of its suspension, but no occupant could be seen through the side windows. The bolder of the two boys wanted to know what was going on, crept up to the car and took a stealthy look through the window. He returned to his friend and said: 'It's just like my Dad said. Not a stitch to her name, but she does have a car.'

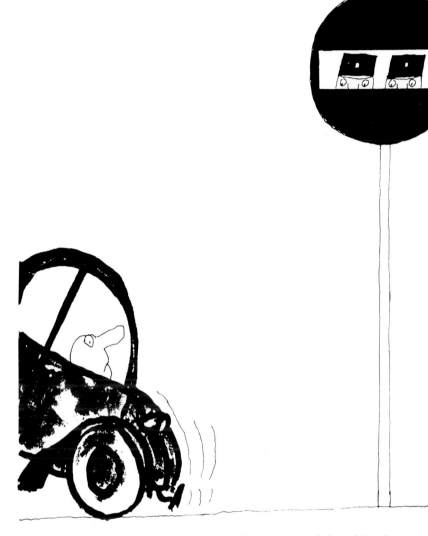

... and that of Desclozeaux.

What's in a name

Every weekend sailor who makes the waterways unsafe in his tub and does irreparable damage to the reedbeds thinks of himself as a skipper under God and names his boat with suitable grandiloquence.

Truck drivers, too, will christen their lumbering monsters, preferably with girl's names. But a respectable car owner does not spoil his paintwork with whimsies of this kind. You never see an Opel, Mercedes or BMW with a personal name on the boot lid.

Here, too, 2CV drivers are an exception. The beloved pet is given a pet name, or is decorated with stickers and drawings, from the most obvious to the most original.

Obvious devices are, of course, the mother ducks with or without a brood of ducklings, or the flying ducks with outstretched wings. A butterfly on the back may indicate the flitting, floating nature of the car, or the fluttering of the lady inside. And a snail painted on the back shows the perpetrator to be possessed of a great capacity for seeing everything as relative.

Far too many people in Holland have called their 2CVs Wammes Waggel, after a character in the work of Marten Toonder, with no thought of paying the copyright fee. Wittier efforts, again in Holland, depend on *eend* ('duck') rhyming with English 'ain't', thus *Eend*

she Sweet and *De Seend*. Then there are *Zontomaatje,* with its pun on 'tomato' for a red 2CV and *Canard à l'orange* for an orange one. 'I demand the emancipation of the duckling' is a fashionable inscription; 'Never a Rolls again' is haughty if not supercilious; and the true 2CV mentality shines through in 'I'm not very fast but I'll get there at last (hopefully)'.

Cartoonist César's classical inspiration.

The farmer, putting his hand to the plough, (drawing by Vetikko).

La realité dépasse la fiction

This saying from the homeland of the 2CV can be rendered as 'Truth is stranger than fiction.' Certainly there are real-life tales about the 2CV that are more amusing, more likely to raise a laugh, than any of the made-up jokes. Many of them derive from the fact that in the early years especially, the 2CV got into the hands of many people who had never had a car before – innocents who were new to the game. Again, Boulanger's foresight is to be commended, with his legendary farmer's wife who would only be confused if you gave her too many knobs and handles to work.

There was the moving story of the two nuns who used a 2CV for their rural social work. On one occasion they told the dealer that they found it an excellent little car, but there were a few practical drawbacks. Topping up the oil was, they thought, a very time-consuming business and to make it easier, they had even bought a little perfume dropper. In response to the dealer's astonished expression they asked him to open the bonnet ... apparently they had been topping up the oil via the dipstick hole.

Then there was the lady at an instruction session who remarked that you could not get much water into the radiator. When the instructor told her that the 2CV was air-cooled and had no radiator she replied that there *was* a cap for it. Evidently she had been tipping buckets of water into the crankcase.

Over-compensation is a familiar human characteristic. The French perfume industry owes a lot to the fact that the Sun King and his court did not wash much and they applied this principle so as to be able to remain in each other's presence. It must have been thinking along these lines that led a 2CV driver, irritated by the noise his car made at higher revs, to blot it out by making a hole in the exhaust and fitting the whistle from a kettle in it. The sound the escaping gases made was like music in his ears, but it brought other road users to the boil.

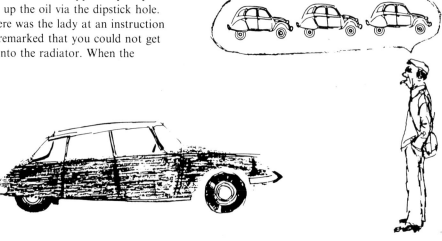

A twelve-seater for the same price (drawing by Kerleroux).

IT TAUGHT US ALL WE KNOW.

It's not all bad being a tortoise. They do live to a very old age.

They suffer few mechanical breakdowns.

They have a very poor appetite for consuming petrol.

They're not, as we know, the swiftest of creatures.

But need we remind you of the story of the tortoise and the hare?

CITROËN 2CV £2774.

Weddings and parties

The forethought of the designers of the 2CV in ensuring that a good-sized man could sit in it with his hat on may be one of the reasons why the car has played such an important part in so many weddings – although the average owner of this vehicle may not usually be the sort to think in terms of morning coat and top hat. The Citroën archives, however, contain an ever-growing number of cards announcing engagements, weddings, births and removals that feature the 2CV in humorous fashion. The cars are depicted full of household effects; on menus announcing duck pâté or breast of duck; photographed carrying the bridal procession; with a cradle behind or a stork above; on the honeymoon trip to India or Lapland. And the plays on words are legion: *'deux heureux';* 'marrying takes two and a 2CV'; 'hooray, we've got another duckling'; 'pitstop at the Town Hall, then we'll get oiled at the reception! The 2CV is commonly involved in all kinds of family occasions and even – though here the humour becomes rather black – in funerals. In Andorra one of them has been in use as a hearse for many years: the back seat and one of the front seats have been taken out to make room for the coffin.

An Amsterdam newspaper once carried a photo on April 1st with the report that the local police, for reasons of economy, had decided to replace their Beetles with 2CVs. They were very

April Fool!

During a check, Dutch traffic police discovered chassis members made of oak on an ancient 2CV – replacing metal that had rusted away.

practical after all: with the hood back you could stand up and direct the traffic. Members of motor units, who had not noticed the date, went to their superiors and angrily protested that they had not been consulted. And anyway, imagine such a conformist person as a cop in a nonconformist conveyance like this!

The 2CV even managed to make it into Carnival. The town of Boxtel takes on the name 'Eendengat' during the days of Carnival, which could be taken to refer to the rear end of a duck. In 1964 the chosen Carnival Prince decided to make the Ugly Duckling his official

limousine in which to make his 'progress' through the town. The car ended up with 20 litres of beer in its tank, which will have rendered its motion even more ducklike.

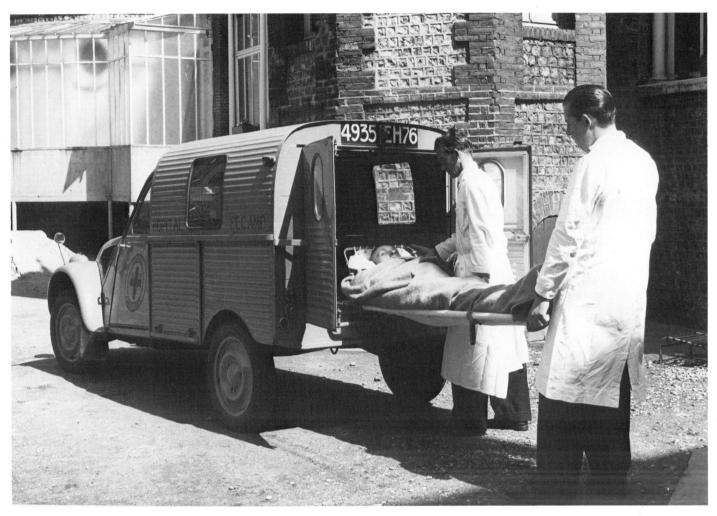

Not the Andorran hearse but a 2CV ambulance – at Fécamp in France, adapted in the same way.

Jolting round Boxtel in Holland at Carnival time.

Opposite above: Wedding 2CV at Haarlem

Opposite below: Ugly Duckling with an odd-looking beak.

This page: You never get this kind of humour from Opel drivers.

The original 2CVs had a dipstick attached to the filler cap instead of a fuel gauge. Careless or absent-minded drivers were apt to run out of petrol on the road. One bright spark had an idea: he cut off a piece of the dipstick so that if it registered 'empty' he knew he still had a gallon or so left.

The 2CV and the cartoonists

A car that has been so undeniably part of our culture for 35 years has naturally been a target for cartoonists. There would be little point in accompanying these cartoons with text – this would be a contradiction of their very essence. That is why a good deal of space has been given in this chapter simply to offering a glimpse of the place cartoonists have given the 2CV in their work. Most of them, of course, have been French, but the Dutchman Wim Boost, with his cartoon spot on the front page of *De Volkskrant,* by no means cuts a bad figure in their company. What is striking is that some of the cartoons derive their humour from things that are actually possible for a 2CV. There is, for example, Daniel Dufour's strip about the window cleaner and his ladder – which was taken from life. Worthy of special note are the coloured prints by the Frenchman Guy Teteau, suggesting how on a journey across Africa the car was able to keep the wild life at bay by mimicking the camel, the lion, the elephant, the hippopotamus, the tortoise or the giraffe.

Opposite above: Cartoon by Beck.

Opposite below: Daniel Dufour drew this sequence from real life.

One 2CV driver in a remote part of France, who found the daily journey to and from work rather too long, discovered that he could shorten it by 12 miles by going to the railway track and rattling along on the sleepers – behind the train, or even ahead of it!

And from Holland cartoons by Wim Boost (Wibo).

A Bird of Passage

The first 2CVs were far from ideal for long journeys. Fully loaded they were difficult to urge forward once you had a headwind of force 6 to 8 on the Beaufort Scale. A steep mountain pass would soon prove too much for these early specimens. Stories abound of families in the Alps or the Cévennes having to unload all their luggage a thousand feet or so from the top of a pass and push out the passengers to struggle uphill with it, while Dad and Mum drove on up in the emptied vehicle, which would then be loaded up again after a hot half hour or so. Sometimes this could happen four or five times in day's travelling.

Some bright sparks discovered that the answer was to turn the 2CV round and go uphill backwards. Apparently the ratios meant that the reverse gear had greater pulling power than the others. Which was all very well – but driving backwards alongside a ravine called for steersmanship of a high order, and a certain defiance of death.

Solitary 2CV on the African Rally (Raid Afrique) *across the Sahara to the Ivory Coast. Other ships of the desert look on.*

39

1971 rally to Persepolis, the ancient heart of Persia.

Opposite: Among the camels in Iran and in the heart of Africa.

Nevertheless there have been hundreds – probably thousands – of drivers who right from its inception have taken up the challenge of long, even round-the-world, journeys in the 2CV: through soft desert sand, dried-up riverbeds and swamps; across upland ridges and along valleys; in the snow above the Arctic Circle or the sweltering heat of Central Africa.

Let us start by picking out just one of these world travellers. The Frenchman Jacques Cornet wore out twelve 2CVs between 1953 and 1968 on roads around the world. Five years after the introduction of 'the great mistake', the era of world journeys by 2CV began with him. Here is his record:

1953 Canada – Tierra del Fuego, back to Franch via the Sahara, 32,300 miles: 375 cc 2CV
1955 New York – Mexico, 12,400 miles: 425 cc 2CV
1956 Paris – Tokyo – Paris, 28,000 miles: 425 cc 2 CV
1960 North Africa – Egypt – Namibia 15,500 miles: 425 cc 2CV
1964 Around Argentina, 15,500 miles: Argentinian-built 425 cc 2CV
1967 Geneva – Teheran – Iranian Gulf – Caspian Sea and back, 11,500 miles: 2CV Azam-6
1968 Iran and Afghanistan, 19,600 miles: Dyane 6

This makes a total of 134,800 miles: imposing figures that nevertheless give little indication of all the hardships and rigours, the moments of fear, surprise and adventure, and the spirit, that lie behind them.

They say nothing, for example, about climbing an icy mountain road near the Caspian Sea in the depth of winter and in darkness only to find the pass blocked by snow and then, as there was no going back, spending the night in the car at a temperature of -30°C (-22°F). Or driving along Afghan cart tracks, on the highest 'road' in the world, often with gradients of 1-in-3 and achieving a daily average of 93 miles only by staying at the wheel for twelve hours at a stretch! An even lower daily average was chalked up by a Dutchman who, for several years running, drove to and around Austria towing a 1320 lb (about 12 cwt) caravan behind his 2CV. When asked in some surprise how he managed it he replied that it wasn't too bad really, but there were days when he did not get out of first gear!

Pelted with stones in Turkey, warmly received (in those days!) in Iran: Paris – Persepolis 1971.

Above right: Eleven-year-old 2CV by the centuries-old Taj Mahal.

Above left: 'A trip around the Mediterranean.'

Below left: Trouble in the desert.

Long drive to Tibet

In 1963 two Dutch students, Arie Prevo and Henk van der Leest, bought a 1952 2CV. In the hard currency of over twenty years ago they paid 500 Dutch guilders for the eleven-year-old car, which already had 87,000 miles on the clock.

Unlike many other travellers who bolt all sorts of gadgets and extras on to their 2CVs before setting out, this pair simply stepped into their ordinary, production 2CV for what was intended as a 'trip around the Mediterranean' an ambitious enough undertaking by any reckoning. A third friend was to have gone with them, but a trial drive fully loaded showed that the 2CV could not manage the weight and so the third man stayed at home. With 800 guilders in their pockets they rattled out of Rotterdam like many voyagers who had left the port before them (with or without the due complement of cockroaches, ship's rats and weevils). No further on than Limburg they had to stop at a garage for repairs, but then they jolted on through Germany, Yugoslavia, Turkey, Iran, Pakistan and India to within 125 miles of the Tibetan border – somewhat further

than they had planned. And then they had to make their way back.

The journey did not, of course, proceed without some wear and tear on the vehicle's fabric. When they set out they had had two new and four old tyres. The treads were not too badly worn, but the sharp stones of the unsurfaced desert roads – and they covered some 4100 miles on these – regularly penetrated the tyre walls and gave them punctures on at least 46 occasions.

Despite so prudently leaving the third man at home, when they saw an American hitch-hiker standing all alone in the desert region between India and Pakistan they could not bring themselves to pass him by. They gave the man a lift for 620 miles. Unfortunately, he was rather stout and one of the wheels gave way in protest – which was hardly surprising as it had been bought from a scrapyard and had fifteen years' service behind it.

Another assault on the 2CV came in Istanbul – from a horse, which sat on one of the front wings. Although they had lived thriftily, often sharing in the scanty meals of the

44

local people on the way, who always came hurrying up in droves when the extraordinary apparition lurched into their village, their money ran out in Pakistan on the way back. By then their journey had already lasted a month longer than anticipated. They sold all their belongings – sleeping bags, camera, tent. They slept in the open, beside the car, or else they took turn and turn about, one driving while the other slept in order to make up time. Although their 2CV no longer had any lights, the wheels were out of alignment because of a damaged chassis, and the steering pulled to one side, they were still able, going downhill and with the wind behind them, to reach a top speed of 75 mph on the German *Autobahnen!*.

Then, after this journey across eight deserts and as far as the Himalayas, through mountain rivers when there was no bridge, and after being waylaid by bandits (the 2CV had bullet holes in its sides), the pair came up against some humourless members of the Dutch Customs at their home frontier. There was a mechanical inspection at Roermond and the two were offically banned from driving the vehicle. A friend took it in tow but the towrope broke opposite Eindhoven and so – oh, the shame of it! – they had to do the very last bit of the journey by train.

From Albion to Araby

Brits are not excluded from epic journeys, one of the most recent being that made by Ashley and Nicola Earwaker of Kent who, in 1985, set off in their 2CV India-bound. A 2CV was bought especially because of its legendary reliability and fuel economy, and was suitably modified with such ex-works parts as special front bumper and air filter and a sump guard and fuel tank guard. Other changes included a home-made bull bar, protective grilles, extra door-locks, and a lockable steel box substituted for the rear seats and bolted firmly to the floor.

A journey through Europe led to Turkey, where the state of the roads progressively deteriorated as altitude increased, and where the 2CV's greatest challenge was encountered – the ascent of the famous Nemrut Dagi mountain (7054ft), at the summit of which is the tomb of King Antiochus I, surrounded by colossal stone statues. The mountain's 26 mile unsurfaced approach track culminates in a slope so steep that, to prevent stalling, the 2CV had to be weaved to-and-fro across the road merely to keep up enough momentum. Within a

hair-breadth of faltering at the last, the 2CV breasted the final rise, only to find already at the top – a Citröen Dyane!

Heading south the next ports of call included Damascus in Syria and Amman in Jordan en route to Saudia Arabia, at which border the 2CV was not only emptied and its contents scrutinized minutely, but was also partly dismantled in a search for alcohol, drugs, arms and pornographic material.

The deserts of Saudi and Qatar were crossed as quickly as is possible in a 2CV in a headwind – four days – during which the pair were reduced to one driver; women at the wheel being prohibited in those parts.

From the shores of Arabia to the Indian sub-continent there is only one way for a Duck to go – by water. Accordingly the 2CV was enshipped at Sharjah for Karachi whilst the *pilotes* went ahead by air.

After some days of struggling with red tape in the form of customs bureaucracy, the 2CV was aimed in the direction of Hyderabad and then Mehar. It was here, still in Pakistan that plans to reach India were violently revised, for in the dead of night the sleeping couple were attacked by intruders. Only after a long struggle was an escape made, with Nicola driving and Ashley, who had collected some shot-gun pellets in one arm, clinging to the bull-bar.

Too shocked and un-nerved to continue their journey the couple eventually found their way home after a total of 9000 miles. And the 2CV: still going strong, having averaged 53.3 mpg!

The Earwaker's 2CV being hoisted aboard for the trip to Karachi.

Eyes shut and foot down.

Raid Afrique *1974 – after tropical rain on the Ivory Coast.*

Afloat on a sea of sand in Tunisia ...

... and somewhere in Upper Volta.

Journey from Brussels to a wedding in Tamanrasset, southern Algeria.

Wedding journey with obstacles

In the early 1960s Citroën of France instigated the Prix Citroën Tour du Monde in order to encourage 2CV Grand Touring. The prize was awarded annually for the longest, most difficult or most original journey. In 1968 the prize went to two Belgians, Elisabeth Gilmont, an economist, and Daniel Gilmont, lecturer in photography. They decided that year to make their wedding journey not after but before and during the event. The building used for wedding ceremonies on the Grand Place in their native Brussels may have been very splendid, but they wanted to be joined in matrimony by a Belgian missionary who for twenty years had been working in southern Algeria, in Tamanrasset at the foot of the Ahaggar Massif. For the priest, Father Charles de Foucault, it would be the first marriage ceremony he had performed in his career. In the meantime the altar was 7500 miles from Brussels. The engaged couple set out in a Dyane 6 on a journey 2500 miles of which lay on sand and rock roads, including hundreds of miles of notorious Saharan caravan routes. These are euphemistically described as

'undulating': in other words, one long washboard on which a 2CV in particular with its singular suspension would pitch and toss like a true ship of the desert. The only method of crossing all this in reasonable comfort was to put your foot down and go as fast as possible leaping, as it were, from ripple to ripple. In the eastern part of the great Erg desert the pair endured temperature differences of 40°C (104°F) and more, climbed over the Tademait plateau – unreclaimed and barely navigable by road vehicles – and arrived in time for the ceremony, having had not a single break-down. That they still wanted to say 'yes' after sharing a journey like this indicates great compatibility – for many existing marriages have failed in car journeys on narrow mountain roads and in similarly miserable conditions.

The young newly-weds honeymooned for several weeks in a Tuareg encampment then returned across North Africa and via Spain back to Brussels: 15,500 miles and an undamaged Dyane!

The most southerly 2CV in the world is in Tierra del Fuego, right down at the bottom of South America. Nuns use it to ferry children to the convent school.

48

Citronetta – an insect repellant?

To some, the name Citronetta conjures up pictures of swarms of dancing gnats or midges on a hot summer evening, or the whining kamikaze dive of one of them in your bedroom – for it is a much used insect repellant in Holland. In Chile, however, a Citronetta is a 2CV from the local Citroën factories. In front it looks like the European 2CV, but at the back it is equipped with a large, box-shaped boot. In one of these remarkable cars, vintage 1960, with 125,000 miles on the clock, and with US $350 travelling money, two firemen set off in 1971 on what can be claimed without any fear of contradiction as the record 2CV world journey. Their first destination was Sweden where, they said, they were going to buy safety matches: once a fireman, always a fireman! There were in no hurry. They travelled through the whole of Chile, then through Peru, Equador and Colombia, Panama, Costa Rica, Nicaragua, Honduras, El Salvador, Guatemala and Mexico. They crossed nineteen American states from the Pacific to the Atlantic, and then with some regret put their Citronetta on board ship. The English Channel may not have been crossed in a 2CV as yet, but New York – Hamburg was quite an effort. In 1974, after driving through Denmark, they finally reached Sweden and a box of the desired matches, whose tops do not fall off when struck and which do not spontaneously ignite.

Their wanderlust, however, did not abate even on the snowy Lapland tundra. They drove on, literally from fire station to fire station. Every evening they would seek out the local fire station, where there was always a bed for two enterprising colleagues. Their $350 had not, of course, lasted out the journey, which had lasted four years so far. As we have seen, however, they were in no hurry and whenever they were short of money they hired out their labour for a while. They were not at all choosy about what they did. In Mexico they were house painters, in California gardeners; but here they also featured as 'bad guys' driving freight wagons in a cowboy film. In New York it was the car that earned the money as an item in a big racing car exhibition (in which of the formulas would a Citronetta compete?). In Germany they worked as chefs, with chili con carne as their speciality, no doubt.

They travelled on through Norway, Finland and Germany and came to France, where the 2CV was given a complete check-up. This showed that, apart from normal maintenance, it needed nothing doing to it after

Major servicing after 150,000 miles.

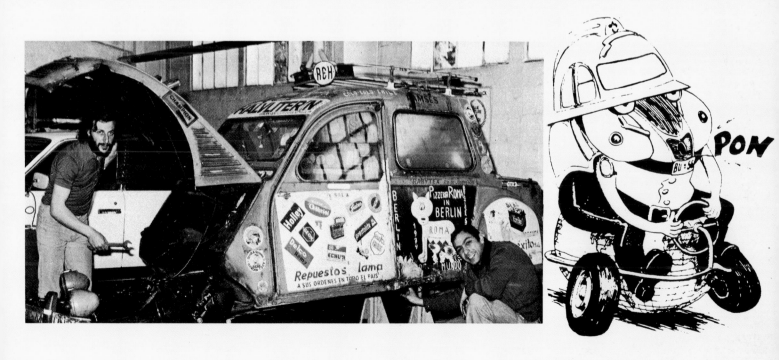

Reindeer encounter.

From Chile to Stockholm for safety matches.

164,000 miles. Once more they set off: Spain, Portugal, Italy, Tunisia, Morocco, southern Algeria, five days across the desert and then they were stranded. Their luggage had grown to the point where the Citronetta was loaded to 550 lb (about 5 cwt) above its capacity. This had finally put paid to the chassis. They had again been earning something on the way, however and they were able to buy an old 2CV for next to nothing. They removed its chassis and installed it in their trusty Citronetta. They journeyed on again, to the Ivory Coast where a few months putting up telegraph poles brought them in some cash. Ghana, Togo, Benin (Dahomey), Nigeria, Cameroon, Zaire and Rwanda Burundi were visited, but this was no flying visit. They purposely spent weeks or months in each area. Fate also took a hand. The Citronetta showed signs of cylinder head

trouble and one of the firemen contracted hepatitis. To make matters worse they were arrested on suspicion (of what? Probably of being alien and therefore a danger to the state) and thrown into jail. The police then handed them over to the army. The military put them in a cell and then handed them back to the police, and so on. Finally they were released, but escorted to the frontier by a couple of formidable armoured cars.

After visiting Kenya, Tanzania, Zambia and Malawi they returned to Paris in 1980. After a thorough overhaul of their steed they departed immediately in the direction of the Yemen, for their Citronetta had not yet seen anything of the middle or Far East. Where the pair are now is not known. We shall no doubt hear more of them when the 50th anniversary of the 2CV comes round!

2CV long-distance 'raid'

For English speakers a raid is primarily a military operation by land, sea or air. But for the French the word – in Franglais – has come to mean a long motor drive. Citroën organized sporting rally-type events early in the history of the motor car. In 1922, for example, five *autochenilles* (half-tracks – Citroën production cars with caterpillar tracks replacing the rear wheels) cross the Sahara from Algeria to Timbuktu. In 1924 the company organized another drive; this time eight of the half-tracks travelled through the whole of the African continent in an event called the *Croisière Noire*. The *Croisière Jaune* ('yellow because it lay through countries inhabited by Mongoloid peoples) followed in 1931, when ten Citroën-Kégresse half-tracks took part. This time, however, the rally ran into problems. In China the participants were accused of sabotage and political agitation, their cars and passports were seized and were only to be returned after a ransom of three Citroëns had been paid. As the cars were then stolen from police custody by rebels and it' took two months for the 'ransom' Citroëns to arrive from Paris and for the purloined cars to be traced, the expedition had to make its crossing of the Gobi desert in December, in a temperature of -33°C (-27°F). Their engine oil froze with the power units ticking over! The *Croisière Jaune* reached Peking, but its leader died there and the return journey was made by ship.

As more and more 2CV drivers were emerging as world travellers, Citroën decided in 1970 to restore the old *croisière* tradition: this time, however, Ugly Ducklings not caterpillars were to be involved.

It was young people in particular who had chosen the 2CV in such numbers and so the factory aimed its new safari, the *Croisière Jeune*, at them. The course chosen was the old Silk Road, along the caravan routes traversed by Alexander the Great and Marco Polo: from Paris to Kabul in Afghanistan and back, a distance of 10,250 miles.

As soon as registration began, applications to take part flooded in from all the countries of Europe where the 2CV was known. Five thousand hopefuls asked for details and this resulted in 1200 provisional entries being registered. Of these 535 were selected, of whom 494 eventually appeared at the start. At Kabul there were still 480 teams left in the event; and 458 made it back to Paris – 320 of them within the stipulated time limit. Out of this number 213 had not so much as had their names and addresses taken on the journey.

The participants had to record an account of their journey on their return, a requirement that produced 16 miles of tape.

In short, the rally was an outstanding success. Belgians, Swiss, Germans, Dutchmen, Spaniards and, of course, very many Frenchmen had taken part. Between checkpoints every competitor could choose his own route and stopping places. When within a few hours of one day a couple of hundred 2CVs rolled into Kabul the town was stood on its head. The police were turned out in full strength and in full dress to deal with the invasion and the participants drove between lines of officials. The 458 cars that arrived back in Paris contained about a thousand young people. That all of them were aglow with enthusiasm and would have liked to start off for some other destination straight away is perhaps not so remarkable. But is it not remarkable that on such an arduous journey along caravan trails and across dried-up rivers the drop-out rate should only have been 7 per cent? A true 2CV enthusiast is inclined to regard this as only normal, but it says a lot for the technological refinement and skill that went into the original design of this rather fragile-looking car.

The 1971 'raid' had as its destination

Persepolis, the ruins, in Iran, of what was once the sacred capital of the great Persian Empire, founded in about 520 BC and plundered and burned by Alexander the Great in 330 BC. Like the soldiers of Alexander before them, but with less hostile intentions, a host of 2CVs now came to disturb the peace around the royal tombs.

In the meantime these rallies were developing a folklore, a mythology, all their own. Few of the 2CVs lining up for the start looked 'normal'. The warpaint varied from simple chequered patterns to psychedelic designs, from military-style camouflage to tiger stripes. One competing Dyane had a thatched roof; another was stuck all over with silver paper as a protection against the sun. Some had armour plating, some chromed exhausts, some engraved brass door handles in antique style, or even blue-and-white bathroom tiles on the floor. One 2CV was even fitted with a complete second storey containing a darkroom and an attic style sleeping space. I have recently seen this particular 2CV driving about Brockenhurst in the New Forest.

In Turkey the teams had to contend with hostility on the part of the population. The cars were regularly pelted with stones and they could not stop without being immediately surrounded by swarms of importunate Turks. Once over the Turkish-Iranian border, however, stone-throwing gave way to flower-strewing. The competitors even complained that the Iranian government had things a little too perfectly organized, so that some of the sense of adventure was lost.

Once again, in spite of everything, a surprisingly high percentage completed the course, but most of the cars were dented and marked by Turkish stones or by none too gentle contact with free-roaming goats, sheep and donkeys.

The most remarkable souvenir was brought back by a team that had also set out with the most unusual mascot: a black hen meant to provide fresh eggs *en route*. To end the poor creature's loneliness the team had found her a mate in Iran, a first-class fighting cock that was borne home in triumph.

How difficult the trip had been at times is indicated by the words that one of the participants wrote on his boot lid on his return: 'What I have performed, no animal in the world could match', a quotation from *The Little Prince,* by the French author and airman Antoine de Saint-Exupéry.

In 1973 the rally went to Africa and the

Paris–Persepolis–Paris: a line on the map, but on the ground hairpin bends all the way.

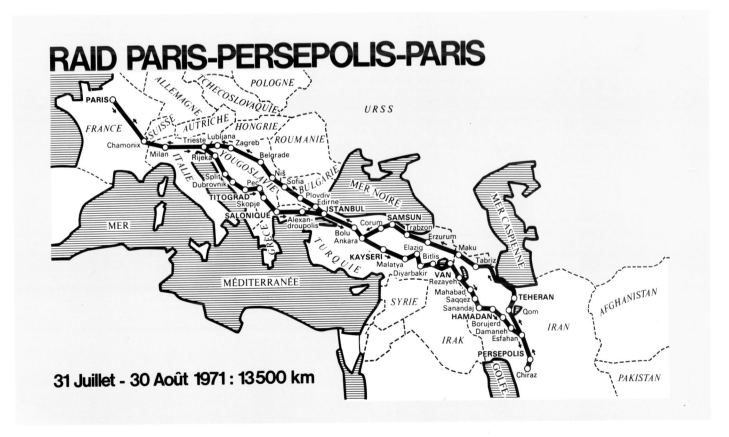

By the Güzelszu fort between Van and Baskale in Turkey.

The same fortress from the other side. Where did those spare tyres suddenly appear from?

Opposite: Still in inhospitable Turkey.

Two-storey 2CV with darkroom.

By the Rungis market halls, Paris, start of the Persepolis rally.

route ran from Tunis through Tunisia, Algeria, Nigeria, Upper Volta to Abidjan on the Ivory Coast and back. Once again there were deserts, trackless mountain wastes, primeval forest, rivers dried up or flooded, hardship – and a lot of fun.

However, even these rallies were becoming somewhat routine and we are not going to describe all of them. One exception we are pleased to make is the 1982 event organized by the Deux Chevaux Club, USA. At first sight this would seem a quite extraordinary club, for the 2CV has been exported to America only in the smallest numbers and is practically unknown there. Nevertheless it was possible to assemble a hundred enthusiasts who had managed to get a 2CV to America – changing the car's status from popular to élite in the process.

To show the 2CV fairly and squarely to their fellow Americans, these hundred fanatics decided to invite a company of Europeans for a rally across the United States, from Los Angeles in a not always straight line to New York City. Not such a long drive this time – a mere 5600 miles in five and a half weeks. The privations, too, were much less than on the 'real' safaris. What was most tiring, perhaps was American curiosity, and the continually repeated question: 'Did you make that car yourself?' However,

competitors from Belgium, Finland, Norway, Switzerland, Britain, the Netherlands (three teams) – and Bahrein! – noted that the drive had had real propaganda value for the Ugly Duckling. For when they arrived at their destination they were able to make quick sales of the second-hand 2CVs for prices between $2000 and $4000.

From the countless exploration journeys, daredevil trips or supertrecks that have been made in these past 38 years we have just picked out a few at random. There is probably no spot in the world (except the South Pole) where some fanatic in a 2CV has not been in the years that the car has been lurching across the face of the earth. We are not, of course, doing all those other travellers justice. Such as, for example, the Dutchmen Bert Becker and Jan Slotboom, who between October 1964 and March 1965 covered 18,600 miles between Amsterdam and India; Dr Wouters, also Dutch, who drove all through Israel and Iran in his 2CV; or his brother who headed for Nepal. Their stories and reminiscences are all well worth hearing – but, alas, there comes a point when we can absorb no more deserts, mountain passes, wadis, 40°C (104°F) temperature differences, or siroccos, and here we must leave it. We believe we have demonstrated that the Ugly Duckling is a true bird of passage.

Kurdish women stare through their yashmaks.

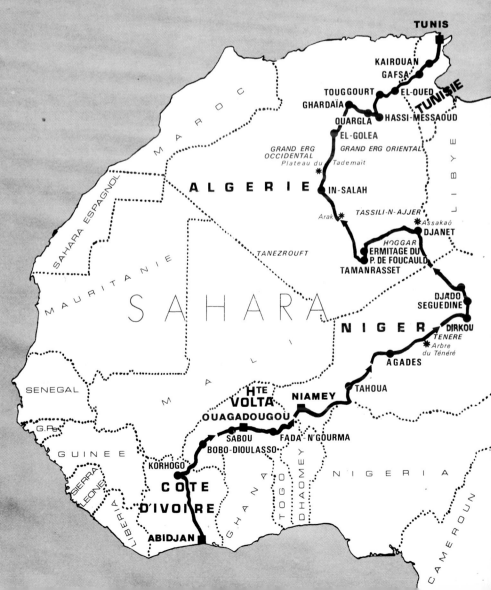

The 1971 rally across Africa.
The desert played nasty tricks,
even on a 2CV.

Algeria, Nigeria, Upper Volta.

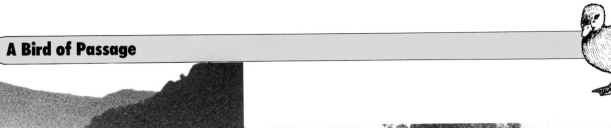

Sahara Duckling

Most of the long-distance journeys described were made in more or less 'normal' 2CVs with a few extras bolted on here and there. In 1958, however, Citroën launched a quite distinct and special heavy-duty version, the Sahara.

That this car had four-wheel drive was in itself no great novelty: Land-Rovers and jeeps were already around in all sorts and sizes. What was absolutely new was the fact that the little car derived its four-wheel drive from two engines – one over the front wheels, the other directly above the rear pair. This type of construction imposed very high demands on the design work. Achieving synchronicity when driving the wheels from one engine is no great problem but doing this with two engines, which have to match exactly in their functioning, requires fine tuning that up till then had not been considered possible. The gearbox, which was also designed specially for the Sahara, had to serve both engines absolutely and precisely simultaneously, but in addition had to be able to work for either of them separately.

That Citroën succeeded in this was shown by the welcome given to the Sahara by professional desert men – police, oil company staff and surveyors. In this context there is a rather nice story about one of these Saharas that had got stuck in soft sand. A Land-Rover was called in to pull it out. The Land-Rover stuck fast in its turn. At this the Sahara driver had the brilliant idea of letting some of the air out of his tyres and this so improved his grip that he was able to tow the rescuing Land-Rover out.

There are convoys and convoys.

The Cultural 2CV

The 2CV is an anarchistic car in the sense that it breaks away from established bourgeois values and makes its own laws. This definition applies to artists, too, for their power lies in either deviating from or particularizing the norm. If they did what everyone else does then their work would lack the distinctiveness that sets it apart as art.

It is hardly surprising, therefore, that there have been many affectionate partnerships between artists and the 2CV and that the car has often been the subject of, or has played a part in, artistic work of all kinds and at all levels.

Artists and acrobats were the first to recognize the Ugly Duckling as an original means of transport. We have already seen that one of the very first owners of the first model was a French actor. It was the same in the Netherlands: the actresses Kitty Courbois and Willeke van Ammelrooy, the drummer Cees See, the artists Gust Romijn, Ans Wortel and Hermanus Berserik, the writer Godfried Bomans and the TV presenter Mies Bouwman all drove around in 2CVs. The founding of the Frysk Orchestra in 1959 was accompanied by a mystery tour through its native Friesland for 2CVs: which was quite natural really, for the car has always been an ideal means of transport for musicians. At one time 25 per cent of Holland's Concertgebouw Orchestra were using them – for what other small, economical car is there that is capable of taking a double bass or a small harp, a harpsichord, two tubas or three cellos? In this brief survey we will take a look at this artistic role of the 2CV.

The public image

In the early years after the introduction of the 2CV on to the Dutch market Citroën thought it desirable to tell new or prospective drivers a little more about the car at information evenings. For this purpose the Utrecht student cabaret performer Johan Noordmans was engaged, as well as a number of experts. This gifted conference entertainer was immensely successful from 1951 to 1955 with his understated, hesitant way of telling jokes. In the course of a 20-minute lesson in front of an audience of 2CV initiates, who were not always noticeably ready with their laughs, he would take the car to pieces. He pointed out that the engine oil had to be changed every 1500 km (930 miles) and that in the gearbox every 5000 km (3100 miles) which, he would say, meant in fact that you should get a new engine every 1500 km and a new gearbox every 5000. That way you could do without all that messy business with the lubrication. He had designed an extension for the front of the 2CV: not only would this make it look more like a car, but you would be home that bit earlier every evening; 'Just work out the difference that would make'. According to him Citroën had been very clever in pitching the price at a level where you said, 'I could just about manage to have a car at that price – but of course this isn't really a car at all'. And so he would go on playing around with the idea of a 2CV. 'The Citroën people tell you how you should clean the car – fine, but they don't tell you how to make it dirty. Never mind, they're commissioning Sartre to write a play about it – *Le Canard Sale*, The Dirty Duckling.'

Opposite: Children at the youth studio of the Musée Beaubourg in the Centre Pompidou, Paris, were given a 2CV project – decorate one of the cars with icing sugar. The result was certainly sweet.

Bert Haanstra's first award-winning documentary film, Spiegel in Holland, consisted entirely of mirror images. This 'reflection of France in Holland' could have been taken from it.

In his painting Hermanus Berserik draws on everyday reality – from which the 2CV cannot be omitted (see also p. 81).

Ans Wortel: her 2CV and its voluptuous curves. (see also p. 81).

Ironically, it was a comedian deprecating the car which finally established it in the affections of the British. True, some thirty years had passed, years in which the car had grown from the corrugated and underpowered 'mobile shed' which Noordmans knew, into a highly efficient small car which Gavin Green of *Car* magazine had praised as staking a very good claim to being 'the best small car ever made'.

The comedian was, of course, Jasper Carrott. In his BBC TV show he admitted that the car he most hated was the 2CV. He went on to explain that it would get in his way on every possible occasion, also, most damningly, it was the car driven by the type of people who became Friends Of The Earth.

People like these, at least according to JC, bought the car on the basis that it helped preserve wildlife. For, his reasoning went, if a 2CV should, in any moment of wildly abberative speed, be unlucky enough to collide with a rabbit, the animal could casually scratch the car from the likely lodging place in its ear with the distainful 'Oh its just another bloody 2CV!'

The overwhelming public reaction to Carrott's diatribe finally nudged Citroën UK, who seemed to have always regarded the 2CV as the type of marketing and merchandising problem they would have wished upon their opposite numbers at Renault, into accepting the cult persona of the car.

While they could ignore the strength of the various 2CV owners' organisations, pay passing lip service to the oddballs who subscribed to 2CV-Cross and make patronising references to the car building some indefinable marque loyalty, Citroën UK had never really capitalised upon the bargain basement end of the range. At least not publicly.

In fact the car had always, on both its first introduction to Great Britain and its subsequent re-introduction in 1975, been advertised as a rough and ready, overtly reliable and overwhelmingly cheap, practical means of transport. A car with as much charisma as a tired railway clerk.

After the media blitz which Carrott gave the car, things had to change. Someone at Citroën UK, probably the marketing manager, John Atkinson, instituted an undersell advertising campaign which rivalled that of the great American VW campaigns of the nineteen-fifties and sixties in impact and far excelled them in terms of talent and originality.

Among the major points of the campaign were the 2CV's advance luxury features. These included central locking, on the basis that no lock was out of reach from the driver's seat, air conditioning, a self evident commodity to all owners, and multi-role functions.

The humorous slant, heavily laden with sympathy, worked wonders. In amongst ads which really had nothing to say, it gained smiles and it attracted the kind of person who felt no need to prove their social standing by driving the latest gadget-laden product of Nagasaki or Wolfsburg.

Possibly, the campaign was helped by the fact that Britain was still reeling from the industrial decline of the late seventies and early eighties. Even if Jasper Carrott's assumption that most of the people who drove them were Friends Of The Earth was slightly wide of the mark, a great number of buyers must have been influenced by the frugality of the car. The fact that the car was classless and had personality in an age of sameness, only added the icing to that particular cake.

Obviously the socially committed would drive such a car. After all, the Weber family from Posy Simmond's popular cult cartoon in the Guardian, had one. Yet the phenomenal growth in the UK market points to a far greater acceptance of the car than could be expected from the smart left intelligensia.

One of the more obvious influences in the rise of the car to popular acceptance must be the amount of motoring personalities, especially journalists, who use the car as personal transport. While the average public perception of the motoring pundit as a pampered semi-celebrity, always on the verge of leaving for or returning from some first class trip to yet another exotic location to test the latest offering from one of the major manufacturers, is somewhat justified, there are those who still rate their own cars in terms of practicality.

Among these can be numbered Peter Nunn, one time assistant editor of *Classic & Sports Car,* who was the first motoring writer to draw attention to the sheer fun of the international meetings of 2CV clubs. By publishing pictures of car-borne custard pie fights and the like, Nunn brought home to many people that to own a collectable 2CV was to enjoy the best of the old car movement while avoiding the tedious aspects which attend the ownership of more expensive machinery.

Staying, for a moment, with the collectors' press, another great 2CV exponent is the editor of *Thoroughbred & Classic Car,* Tony Dron. A successful racer in the minor formulae and in saloons, Tony has indulged a passion for 2CV motoring since the car was reintroduced to the UK market in 1975.

Dron's first 2CV saw service for two years as racing car tug, occasional camera car for *Motor* and all-round general hack. The present car, which must count as one of the most written about examples in the world due to its appearance in the 'Our Cars' slot, was bought by his parents in 1975 and is his 'second' car after the T-Series Bentley, another car which regularly features in the same part of the magazine.

Perhaps Tony was lucky to inherit the car, for one of his favourite 2CV anecdotes concerns the time that the car was almost written off by a herd of cows whilst being driven by his

parents. The incident happened in a narrow country lane when a herd of these usually placid creatures were spooked by a car coming in the opposite direction. In the resulting stampede some £800 worth of panel damage was sustained by the car while the occupants suffered little more that total bemusement.

Car is a magazine which has built an enviable reputation over the years as being both extremely well informed and exceptionally glamourous. To find it as a haven for 2CV drivers is therefore something of an eyebrow raiser, yet both Steve Cropley, the editor, and Gavin Green his colleague, are avid 2CV fans.

For Gavin Green the practicality of the car, coupled with the facility of being able to open the roof on sunny days is his main reason for ownership. For Steve Cropley the same considerations apply, although his own car has been slightly modified in the performance department by the addition of a turbocharger.

Other considerations which make the car so ideal for drivers with access to far more exotic conveyances must be those bound up with the anonymity of the vehicle. Anyone who has passed a police car in any car redolent of performance knows that the notebook will be out and details taken forthwith for even a minor infringement of the speed limit. It would be a brave traffic cop who risked the derision of the court by bringing in the driver of a 2CV!

Likewise, while the owners of more expensive machinery live in dread of the lout who lurks waiting to scratch 'envy stripes' into the side of their prize possession, the owner of a 2CV risks only the unknowledgeable thing slashing the roof if he can't force the door locks.

It is hard to say which of these factors was uppermost in the mind of former French prime minister Laurent Fabius when he chose a 2CV as his personal transport, probably a combination of all; while one assumes that a combination of practicality and convenience led Ford Sierra designer Uwe Bahnson to install one at his chateau.

Former Ferrari Grand Prix driver Jonathon Williams obviously subscribes to the practicality for his need, for speed is catered for by a fleet of high powered motorcycles at his house in southern France. Even so an interview published in *Motoring News* in 1985 described him as driving his 2CV with 'great verve'.

A cultural link with Britain's higher art forms was forged when Dr Johnathan Miller used a 2CV. Somehow the picture of him buzzing back and forth between directing opera and shooting such fine TV programmes as 'The Body In Question', seems totally apt. At one point he was even filmed in the car in the series.

Perhaps one day someone with the talent and time to do so will work out just why this car attracts so many varied personalities from the media world, in the meantime it remains as anarchic in the nineteen-eighties as it was in the early fifties.

Citroën UK's successful advertising campaign was based on a keystone of understatement.

2CV theatre – travelling players of l'Unité et Cie (see also p. 73) performing Proust on the esplanade of the Centre Pompidou, Paris.

Opposite: David Sparrow won the 3rd Photographic Olympic Games with his series of photographs depicting his favourite car.

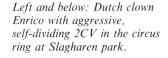

Left and below: Dutch clown Enrico with aggressive, self-dividing 2CV in the circus ring at Slagharen park.

The stage

For the 2CV on the stage, or rather the stage in the 2CV, we do have to go to France. The area in the heart of Paris where Les Halles once stood is now occupied by buildings that include the Centre Pompidou, popularly the Centre Beaubourg. This is a futuristic structure housing a museum of modern art and artists' studios. On the large square in front of the new centre a whole range of 'festival of fools' activities has sprung up. In fine weather dancers and mime artists, fire eaters, jugglers, sword swallowers and clowns desport themselves there and complete mini-dramas are performed. The standard is high. France has never known a system of subsidized theatre of the kind that is now rapidly crumbling away in the Netherlands. Unemployment among actors is high and so, therefore, is the level of inventiveness; and any false modesty about going round with the collecting box in times of need does not last long. The professional theatre group l'Unité et Cie came up with the idea of fitting the rear of a 2CV with a red velvet backcloth and marbled wood wings. Two genuine stalls seats from the Comédie Française were stowed away in the 2CV. These are set up in the street before a performance for the use of honoured guests (i.e. people who have put a goodly sum in the hat). The 2CV acts as changing and make-up room. The actors emerge through the red curtain and stand out on the street. They also act as doormen, usherettes and statutory fireman – all fancy names for collectors. In 1980 they played *l'Odyssée des mulots du lac* (The Odyssey of the Water Voles), an eight-minute solo based on Proust. They do not restrict themselves to the esplanade of the Musée Beaubourg. They took their travelling theatre to the Avignon festival in 1980, where they set up shop in front of the former papal palace.

On an even smaller scale, the puppeteer Philippe Genty turned his 2CV into a travelling theatre. Back in 1950 he started to tour the world with his Ugly Duckling full of puppets. In five years he covered 81,000 miles, and even put on his show in Red Square, in the shadow of the onion domes of the Kremlin.

In 1955, sponsored by Citroën, he travelled around his native France giving an account of his journeys in towns and villages. That is to say, the puppets told the story with Genty's hands pulling the strings. The puppets had their own little 2CV – again with remote (i.e. two-finger) control.

Opposite: Puppeteer Philippe Genty with his leading player and 2CV in Istanbul and Moscow.

From the UNICEF mobile health team centre in Singapore 60 2CV cars and vans transport children's doctors and nurses into the most inhospitable regions of the Far East.

Poster for the James Bond film For Your Eyes Only, *in which a 2CV shared the lead with 007. Right: Suspense sequence from the same film. (see p. 81).*

74

Entries from a competition set by Citroën in 1966-7 for 2CV models constructed out of competitors' own hobby materials. Above left: Spanish grandeur; below left: romanticism; above right: moon lander; below right: semi-precious stones (see p. 83).

Literature

Although during the adolescent years of the 2CV, members of the 'Fifties' group were often in Paris, where Simon Vinkenoog rode between the tables of the Select on the Boulevard Montparnasse, poetry brought in insufficient even to run a 2CV. These poets had to hitchhike, and that must be the reason why none of them mentions the car in his poetry. Bertus Aafjes made the journey to Rome on foot, which cannot have been due to affluence, and the sonnet writer Jan Kal cycled up Mont Ventoux as did Tim Krabbe – although this was a kind of athletic mania rather than poverty. So it was fortunate that Kees Stip enabled the 2CV to make its entry into the Valhalla of Dutch poetry:

> A flea of taste stood quite by chance
> Before some showroom cars in France.
> 'Oh Santa Claus,' the flea did plead,
> 'Give to the cat on whom I feed
> A Renault Quatre, and to me
> For a Christmas gift a 2CV.'

(Dutch words published in *De Volkskrant* newspaper under the pseudonym Trijntje Fop.)

An effort by the German graphic artist Heinz Dorr could also be regarded as literary. For a taxi operator who was using 2CVs at reduced charges he designed a poster based on the lines of a La Fontaine fable, in this case the stork and the Ugly Duckling. In it we see how the stork (representing the more luxurious end of the taxi business) gets angry because the Ugly Duckling keeps dabbling in his particular waters. The following anecdote arising out of this business is alleged to be true: a lady who made use of one of these mini-taxis was charged a mini-fare of DM3.5 She added a tip of DM1.5 saying: 'I'm giving you a bit extra because I think it was so clever of you to have made your taxi all by yourself'.

Without wishing to make any claim to comprehensiveness the 2CV appears, for example, in many detective stories (in which the sleuth conspicuously wants to remain inconspicuous), in spy novels (in which the secret agent has to undertake cross-country rides in competition with big American saloons that are much less suitable for the work) and in thrillers (in which a Deux Chevaux ends up hanging by two wheels from a 300-foot cliff above a raging sea), we believe that one of the most distinguished literary positions the Ugly Duckling has ever occupied is in a little book by L.F. Céline, *Entretiens avec le Professeur Y*

(Conversations with Professor Y). In this work Céline tells the story of Blaise Pascal (1623 – 1662), the French scientist, mathematician and philosopher, who began by turning his back on the Catholic faith, but in 1654 he returned to the bosom of Mother Church, after falling out of his carriage in an accident on one of the bridges over the Seine and spending some frightened moments in the watery depths beneath. Céline continues: 'I would like to see Pascal in a 2CV, going from Le Printemps to the Rue Taitbout! ... then he would no longer be afraid of an abyss! We can no longer live on the surface! ... that is the simple truth.'

Films and photos

For years now the Ugly Duckling has had important roles in the film industry, both in front of and behind the camera. The latter role is by no means unimportant, for it derives directly from the car's unique characteristics: flat floor, rollback open top and perfect roadholding over unexpected bumps. In Holland it was used, for example, by Fons Rademakers as a camera car for filming *Als twee druppels water* (Like Two Drops of Water), by W.F. Hermans. And also for the film of Jan Blokker's *Een avondjurk op de achterbank* (An Evening Gown on the Back Seat); there the author describes the following scene:

> Indeed, what should come driving across the Boulevard de la Croisette escorted by four motorcycle police? A Deux Chevaux! And who was inside it? Vadim. At that time he had just left Bardot, or Bardot him – which is really not my business. In any case Vadim was in the 2CV in his function as film maker – he was kneeling beside the driver and looking back at a tall man operating a film camera on a tripod and giving him instructions. The cameraman was standing where the back seat would be for normal people, the roof was open, of course, and the camera stuck out high above the car. Now, of course, you know the kind of sequence they were shooting and what it looks like in a film. We see hero and heroine in a maddeningly chic sports car screeching along the Riviera. We see them in close-up. We hear one say, 'Happy, darling?' The other answers, with rapturous eyes, 'Oh it's beautiful here!' And once this sentence has been uttered the camera follows their gaze

and we see, through their eyes as it were, the boulevard, the sea, the haute-couture, in short, we see the whole Côte de'Azur pass by. But the next time you see a bit of film like this you may be sure of one thing: it wasn't shot from that chic sports car; it will have been taken from the inevitable 2CV. For the Deux Chevaux is rock-steady on the road – its floor is a self-levelling device for the film camera. You will understand how I used to sit myself behind the wheel after that encounter with Vadim. You just couldn't help thinking, 'I've got the right car, so it won't be long now before I'm making a film with BB.'

The 2CV's roles in front of the camera have been by no means inconsiderable. We must confine ourselves to a few spectacular examples from a long list of leading or important supporting roles. In 1982 the late lamented Louis de Funès, that most French of all Frenchmen, used two 2CV Méharis for *Le Gendarme et les Extra-terrestres. Le Gendarme et les gendarmettes,* also made in 1982, had two Ugly Ducklings and a Méhari, which had as

important a part as de Funès himself. However, by far the most important starring role for a 2CV in recent years was in the 1981 James Bond film *For Your Eyes Only;* on the poster the car was shown driving between the world's most beautiful – albeit heavily armed – female legs. At least four 2CVs were worn out in the process, but then Roger Moore was not exactly gentle with them. In this film 007's partner was the French actress Carole Bouquet, a great crossbow champion – a somewhat anachronistic weapon transported about in a 2CV – while Bond of course drove around in something glossier. After a mysterious murder in a swimming pool 007 manages to escape under cover of 150 girls in bi- and mono-kinis. But before he can get to his car it blows up. Bond gets into the 2CV with his partner. Naturally a chase by the opposition ensues, with the pursuers in much faster cars. To avoid an oncoming bus at the very last minute, Carole drives her 2CV straight at a wall and the car overturns. Villagers standing around put the car the right way up again and it speeds off, this time with James Bond in person at the wheel.

'At all events, Vadim was riding about in that 2CV in his function as film maker ...'

*Results from a schools
competition set by Citroën
Nederland in, 1972 on the
topic 'The car in traffic'.*

Flying 2CV with James Bond (or a stuntman) invisibly at the wheel. Visible – the astonished villain.

Roger Moore doing it himself.

The pursuit is continued, with the evildoers gaining on the 2CV. Bond jams on the brakes and the car spins round 180 degrees and roars off in the opposite direction, thus gaining a lot of ground as the big American cars driven by the pursuers cannot turn so quickly. Bond drives the 2CV off the road, goes like a madman through an olive grove scraping the trees on the way, rattles down a hill and picks up so much speed that he takes off and clears a sunken road just at the moment his pursuers are passing underneath. When the villains try to emulate the 2CV's leap in their huge car they crash. Bond triumphs again, of course. So who is going to take on the 2CV? No one; so it has won once more!

Away from the glamour of 007, the 2CV has recently starred in its own show, a one hour documentary for Channel 4. The brainchild of producer/director Jeremy Llewellyn-Jones, himself a 2CV owner, the film dwells mainly upon the technical virtues of the car. Even so, the affection of all those concerned shines through. A fitting tribute.

The role of the 2CV in photography in the last 35 years requires a separate study: just for this book we had to select from thousands of the most beautiful, the maddest, the most remarkable pictures. One picture we would like to draw special attention to is '2CV Under Snow' with which the Dutch photographer Arnold Lutz scored highest points in the annual World Press Photo exhibition at The Hague in 1968. According to the photographer this was his own 2CV which he found one morning looking like the Abominable Snowman. After taking the photo he wiped some snow away from the door handle, got in, started up and drove away.

Paintings and decorating

The 2CV has been decorated and painted, drawn, reproduced in every material from hardwood to gold and silver, depicted on lino and woodcuts, silkscreen and monoprint – the reader can complete his own list. Artists who have elevated their own 2CVs to works of art often score high in this context, but undoubtedly the world's most beautiful example of the car is that of the Dutch painter and writer Ans Wortel. The theme – rightly – is love and the great inventiveness of the scheme lies in the way that the artist has painted the voluptuously rounded front mudguards and rear wings in a flesh colour, so that the car is no longer a machine but appears to be of desirable flesh and blood. It is not surprising, therefore, that the two prone naked figures on the sides run appreciative hands over the curves. Adam and Eve embrace like two flower-power children on the bonnet, emphasizing the innocence of the owner's love for her 2CV.

Equally sensual was the approach of the French artists Yves and Antoine Saint-George, who painted their 2CV (freely) after Rubens. On the right-hand side three very ample Rubens nymphs dance invitingly; on the other side a bacchanal is under way, with satyrs being not indifferent to willing bacchantes.

The Parisian scene painter Bruno Miliau decorated his car to look like the tomb of Tutankhamun, with brilliant hieroglyphs and miniatures of Ancient Egyptian flute players with tunics, Egyptian profiles and raven-black hair. He executed the painting using classical Japanese and Chinese lacquer techniques, so that the Far and Middle East are brought together on his Dyane.

In decorating their cars the French seem to be inspired by classical or Renaissance works. There is a 2CV driving around Strasbourg with a Michelangelo on the boot lid, various old masters on the doors, with a more contemporary work only on the bonnet: a reproduction of a tapestry by Jean Lurcat.

Roger Frezin, however, is an abstract painter who in 1970 had an exhibition in Lille. In his canvasesm Citroën models and parts recurred continually as elements in his compositions, and the complete 2CV he had painted for the Belgian singer and poet Raoul de Godeswaersvelde was also on display.

Pride of place for painting 2CVs on his canvases goes to the Dutch artist Hermanus Berserik. Of him the Oosthoek encyclopaedia remarks: 'His theme is the reality of everyday, but he endows this with a new perspective by juxtaposing objects in a manner that is not everyday, making use of a great variety of technical means to do so. Sewing machines, sweet jars, model ships, oil lamps and bicycles are frequently recurring motifs in his work.' Before the next edition of the Oosthoek comes out the experts should go and have another look at Berserik's work: the 2CV should not have been omitted from their list!

There are, too, artists who perhaps do not depict the 2CV in their work, but who fill their sketchbooks with what they see through the windows of one – often on the move. During the 2CV African rally described in Chapter 3, the graphic artist Georges Popovitch made gouaches and pen and ink sketches of animals in their natural environment that would otherwise have been inaccessible. Truly an artistic safari!

In the UK the artistic movements have tended to ignore the 2CV. True, there are the occasional psychedelic exercises, a very noticeable example being often seen in Chelsea's Kings Rd. In the main, however, homage to the 2CV has taken the form of handicrafts rather

Winning photo by Arnold Lutz: 2CV under snowy blanket (World Press Photo 1968).

Bricked-up 2CV; 2CV with fairy tales and shower unit: troubadour 2CV with treasure chest.

Tea For Two ... CV. Art or design from Andy & Tamsin Ceramics?

than any attempt to transform the car into a mobile show piece.

In the past few years there has been a plethora of ceramic ornaments and oddments built about the theme of the car. These have included tea pots, storage jars and ashtrays, some in fanciful caricature form, others in fairly graphic representational guise.

Obviously it is a matter of opinion whether these should be regarded as models or interior design artifacts rather than object D'art. Similarly there is a case for arguing that in their appearances in the cartoons of Posy Simmonds and Ralph Honeysett, the cars are featuring in art. In the meantime it must be assumed that the car has never attained the level of functional fashionability in the UK which it has occupied for some decades on mainland Europe.

The modelling arts

There is no material so odd or so strange that you cannot fashion some form of homage to the 2CV from it. The Limburg ceramic artist M. Geilenkirchen made a very fine sequence of pieces that started with a complete egg, from which an Ugly Duckling emerged in six stages. And bronze? The young French sculptor Marital Hetier cast one in this material. Clay? Folke Gotesson, a Swedish potter settled in Stoke-on-Trent in the English potteries, made a whole series of remarkable and imaginative visions of the 2CV – as an aircraft, an armoured vehicle, a Formula 1 machine and so on. So far this has been an incomplete list of models that have been the spontaneous work of the artists concerned. What would happen if Citroën itself set a competition for 2CV models in whatever hobby material the participant chose was revealed in 1966 and 1967. This competition was in fact held in Zurich, Basel, Paris and Amsterdam successively and the results were staggering in both their quantity and quality. The models appeared in the form of a wire cage with real budgerigars inside; others were made of chicken feathers, twigs, corks, bark, knitting, crochet work, music paper, dried flowers, the soles of shoes, soapstone, matches, cigar bands, shells, radio components, bread, silver paper, embroidery. There were abstract 2CVs made, for example, from a chessboard with two horses; from a sardine tin with the appropriate key to open the roof; 2CVs from keys welded together; 2CVs on bedsprings to illustrate the suspension; a 2CV as the jawbone of an ass. There were 2CVs from wood shavings, watch parts, leaded glass, machine parts with ballbearings as wheels, macramé with thimbles as headlamps, an ambulance 2CV with elastoplast rolls for wheels, 2CVs decorated with mother-of-pearl buttons with the handles of a pair of pocket scissors representing the headlamps, a 2CV made from postage stamps, from a canned chicken tin, a 2CV woven out of piping material, one made from cigarette stubs, a bewitched 2CV, one made out of coins (no longer legal tender), one shaped from chicken wire and occupied by indoor plants, one comprised of semi-precious stones, a fairy tale 2CV complete with good and bad fairies, a moon landing 2CV, one made from old turfcutter's shoes, an Art Deco 2CV that could be used as a table lamp ... in short no jury in the world would have been competent to pick the best out of all these objectively. One thing, however, that all these strange downright daft models did show was the blind love that 2CV drivers have for their cars. For the surprising irony pervading the work sent in can only be explained by love. Only someone who has become suffused with, and totally grown into, love like this can stand back and look at it in this way.

Ugly Duckling hatching out – three pieces from a series by the Limburg ceramic artist M. Geilenkirchen.

This streak of behaviour obviously translates extremely well as it crosses the channel. Not only has Britain produced the aforementioned ceramic 2CVs but it has introduced to the world the concept of the cuddly 2CV.

Designed by Bob MacQueen with production expertise courtesy of his wife Karen, the cars are fabricated from felts of varying colours. Like the rear thing they are extremely resilient, and, again like the real thing, they attract children like a jam pot draws wasps.

On a more serious level, or at least more professional, Dave Stride has recreated each evolution of the 2CV in miniature. Although a professional model maker, this series was very much a labour of love as he himself is a keen 2CV owner.

Elsewhere, such items as biscuit cutters, cake tins and even toffee moulds, have allowed the true faithful the chance of creating their own edible models.

Graphic arts

The greatest achievements per square millimetre in this area undoubtedly come from the designers of postage stamps. The highest accolade that can be awarded to an industrial object is for it to appear on a stamp. This artistic and political honour has twice come the way of the 2CV. In 1958 a stamp was issued in France and Algeria bearing a charity surcharge (5 francs on a 15 franc) in favour of the Red Cross. On it a 2CV van of the French PTT was depicted, in green and brown for France, and in orange for Algeria. The hundredth anniversary of the birth of André Citroën was marked by the postal authorities in Mali and Gabon by the simultaneous issue of a series of stamps showing famous Citroën models. The 200 franc stamp carried a picture of the 2CV prototype (200 Gabon francs were worth 5 French francs, but it was an honour none the less).

From a great deal of quite exceptional graphic work devoted to the 2CV we would mention the phenomenal pen and wash drawing by Renate Schwarz showing an Ugly Duckling and a Dyane driving over a rainbow, and the series in pen and coloured ink entitled, in medieval style, *Les Grandes heures de la 2CV*. In this series a simulated woodcut technique was used to depict great moments in 2CV history:

winning the Argentine GP in 1961 (out of 205 cars of all makes, the four 2CVs were the only four to finish); the introduction of the 2CV at the 1948 Paris show in the presence of the then president, Vincent Auriol; the setting up by two young Frenchmen of the world altitude record for cars – 17,780 ft on Mt Chacaltaoya in Bolivia; the 2CV truck in service with the British army – lighter than any other cross-country vehicle, it was particularly suitable for transport by helicopter; the incredible story of the two world travellers whose 2CV ran out of oil in Chile's Atacama desert after their crankcase had sprung a leak – there they stuck until a local Indian stuffed the crankcase with peeled bananas and the engine worked perfectly again (we now know why bananas are curved – to fit into small crankcases); the 2CV's overall victory in the 1959 Caltex Economy Test, conducted over 1240 miles through six countries and in all kinds of conditions, with a fuel consumption of 1/26.7; the remarkable rescue in the harsh winter of 1962-3 of swans frozen into

the IJsselmeer – only the Dutch *Wegenwacht* (AA) men with their 2CV vans were able to drive over the ice and feed the birds; or the grand ceremonial moment when Maharajah Kumar of the little mountain country of Sikkim, bordering on India and Tibet, dedicated his new state limousine – a 2CV, chosen because of the nature of the roads in his realm. This truly brilliant series of pictures was produced on the occasion of the 25th anniversary of the 2CV and now, over a decade later, some of them are reproduced on pages 14 and 15.

Opposite: Two 2CV stamps, from Gabon and France.

Romatic print by Renate Schwarz – 2CVs on a rainbow.

Two Hanover interior designers with their work: a desk-cum-bookcase-cum-bar 2CV. It does everything except go.

Children building a tower from written-off 2CVs at the RAI exhibition building, Amsterdam.

Interior design

There is little call for a car inside a house, but there are occasional points of contact between the 2CV and interior design. There is an interior designer in Hanover who has a complete 2CV in her living room. It is made of wood in fact, but it differs from the real thing in just one respect: it does not go. However, the headlamps flash when the telephone rings, a bookcase is concealed in the boot, the doors open out to form work surfaces, there is a fridge under the bonnet with a tank for whisky, the front wheels can be turned up to serve as bar stools and the inside of the car is a projection room for films and slides, with the frosted glass windshield as a screen. 'Kitsch' would, of course, be a better subheading for this particular item. However, interior design at a much more serious level is also involved. At an exhibition of 50 years of furniture for sitting on, held at the Stedelijk Museum, Amsterdam, in 1966, the 2CV's front seat was found worthy of inclusion in the

definitive selection. This honour was in fact continued when the seat became part of the permanent collection at the Museum of Modern Art, New York.

Children's art

Every Citroën is a family car. André Citroën himself declared, 'I want the first three words that children are able to say to be "Mummy", "Daddy", "Citroën". Today we might find this pronouncement just a little too commercial, but it could be paraphrased as, 'I want the children on the back seat to be just as happy in my cars as their parents on the front seat'. Be that as it may, over the years Citroën has organized many events that centre on the child. There have been one-day events, such as the workshop at the RAI exhibition centre in Amsterdam, where a

86

number of wrecks were put at the disposal of the children with the invitation to make something from them. The result was a heap of 2CVs, a whimsical memorial to multiple pile-ups. Then there was the task set for children at the creative youth studio of the Musée Beaubourg, Paris. They were given 660 lb of confectioner's icing in the whole range of acid-drop colours and told to decorage a 2CV. The result may not have been elegant, but it was certainly sweet.

In 1972 Citroën Nederland sent out to all the country's primary schools for drawings on the theme 'The Car in the Traffic'. The competition did not stipulate that the car had to be a 2CV, or even a Citroën. Thousands of pictures flooded in. Often they were drawings made from the back seat and offering a view of a Holland that was crowded and busy, full of accidents, tail-backs and air pollution – but also full of holiday pleasures. The jury picked out '50 very good ones', for selecting the '50 best' seemed not only unfair, but also impossible. These 50 good ones were brought together in a book that preserves the original directness of the children's work – although the artists themselves have by now grown up, or nearly so. The book includes accompanying letters, such as:

Dear mr citrun,
I am writing you a letter all citruns are yellow which is right because a citrun [= 'lemon'] is yellow. So it is true.
Goodbye mr citrun

Dear mr citroën director,
Perhaps I will get a prize I dont know yet. Miss says I have done a nice picture but the roads are full of cars TOOT-TOOT from Atsen.

In Italy the youth publication *Corriere dei Piccoli* set a similar competition, but with the title 'Give your father and mother a 2CV as a present' and with the instruction that the children should design the decoration for the car. A 10-year-old boy won the competition with an amazing design. In it 'two horsepower' was visualized literally, with two horse's heads facing each other on the boot lid and the outline of two horses on the canvas roof (for people on upper floors and truck drivers to enjoy).

In 1982 children at the youth studio of the Musée Beaubourg were again set to work on a 2CV project. This time they were given plastic models of the body and with this as a base, and using any conceivable kind of material, they had to devise a 2CV suitable for a journey through primeval forestry on swampy ground. Their work had to be accompanied by a written explanation. The very imaginative 'instructions for use' from one of the prize winners, a girl of about ten, ran as follows:

We live in a country. There is only tropical forest with lianas and undergrowth and it is muddy and swampy. I hear a sound. Quickly I pick it up on the aerial and it is a lion. I open the trap behind the car. He has been taking the food there and because there are sleeping tablets in it he falls asleep and the five of us get away. Suddenly we see huge hedgehogs in the way, but fortunately I have

Make your own 2CV – and make up a story to go with it. Youthful creativity at the Centre Pompidou, Paris.

The very successful 2CV Charleston, accentuating the 'Bauhaus' circle again. Nostalgia is 'in'.

Limewood carving made by the designer Karel Suyling. Plastic reproductions of this mascot were to dangle behind the rear windows of tens of thousands of 2CVs for years to come.

In 1957 the first car to drive on the still soft ground of the newly reclaimed East Flevoland polders was a 2CV. Since then the 2CV has been the favourite vehicle with the Dutch government department for canals, dikes, bridges and roads, which uses it for transport around unreclaimed polders.

my feather in the car and I tickle their feet so that they creep away and do not puncture the tyres. I begin to feel a bit hungry, but look, I am right beneath a coconut tree! With my pincers I get hold of a coconut and work it loose so it drops in my net. Dusk begins to fall and I have to turn the headlamps on so that the animals outside cannot see in but we can see out. And if we are thirsty there is a tank so that we can have a drink. But look out, we're sinking! Quick, we must use out fantastic mud brooms which sweep the mud away so that we can drive on, but now I get a lump of mud in my face so we must be careful.

Design

Design is a word the meaning of which is not easy to define: it covers everything. We are using it here rather as a translation of the French term *l'art décoratif*, but this, too, is somewhat vague and imprecise.

The term could include the decorated 2CVs described earlier; but it applies more to the kind of decorative effects that lend themselves to series production rather than individualistic expressions of individual feelings. A typical sample of 2CV design is the Charleston model that has become so popular. This version, sprayed black with a second colour of, for instance, maroon, accentuates the 'Bauhaus' circle of the doors once more. A rather splendid example of this kind of thing came from a student at the Ecole Camondo, a French industrial arts college. Given a project to style a 2CV as a basketball shoe, he came out with one that had laces and laceholes on its bonnet. This design, not in series production as yet, achieved further fame by appearing in the Paris Cirque d'Hiver. As most viewers of Continental television know there is an annual charity performance, the Nuit des Etoiles, at this winter

circus. In it professional artists from other media put on circus acts. A few years ago Michel Legrand, the composer, arranger, conductor and singer responsible for 'The Windmills of my Mind' did a lion-taming act. However, being nervous of beasts of prey, he substituted a Basketball Shoe 2CV for the lions. This he attempted to subdue, while the monster tried to kick him out of the ring. Laughs, roars and growls abounded – it was certainly an act worth seeing.

The discussion takes on a more serious note when we turn to graphic design. For Citroën the general rule in this field has been to show the 'company image' in the most progressive light possible. Just as all Citroën cars have always been in advance of their time and have demonstrated the courage of their designers and makers in terms both of technology and appearance, so too in its graphic design the company has consistently been a pioneer. It was only right, therefore, that in the early 1970s the Musée des Arts Décoratifs in Paris and the Department of Applied Art of the Stedelijk Museum, Amsterdam, should have held a special exhibition, 'An Enterprise and its Publicity: Citroën', on the subject of the company's graphic design. In the catalogue to the exhibition René Salanon, chief librarian at the Musée des Arts Décoratifs, wrote:

> In all ages the mighty of this world, whether in the field of politics or arms, of trade or money, of the intellect or of religion, have engaged artists to praise their merits, to sing of their power, to serve their interests. In no period in the past, however, has there been so large and important a distribution of the publicity media as in our own time. Everyone who has anything to sell makes use of them; large corporations commission work and in so doing take on the role of the real or presumed Maecenases of the past.

To which Wil Bertheux, the curator of Applied Arts at the Stedelijk Museum added:

> The Citroën company, which has contributed greatly to the enhancement of our environment with good design, has followed this same course in its publicity. Its commissioning of work in this area gives evidence of its desire to put quality first. Robert Delpire, André François, William Klein and François Reichenbach are names that as good as guarantee amazingly fine results.

The exhibition, and some of the reproductions in this book, show the truth of these words. However, simple justice requires the addition of a few Dutch names to the list. The exhibition typified French centralizing tendencies in being based solely on the activities of the parent

JAAP VEGTER

Strip 2CV. Cartoon by Jaap Vegter that appeared in Vrij Nederland *newspaper on 22 August 1981.*

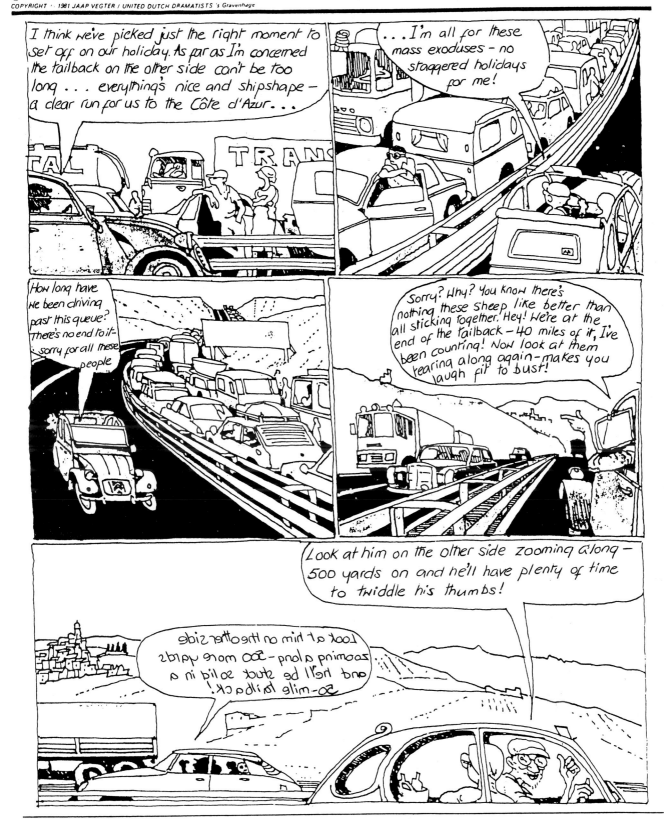

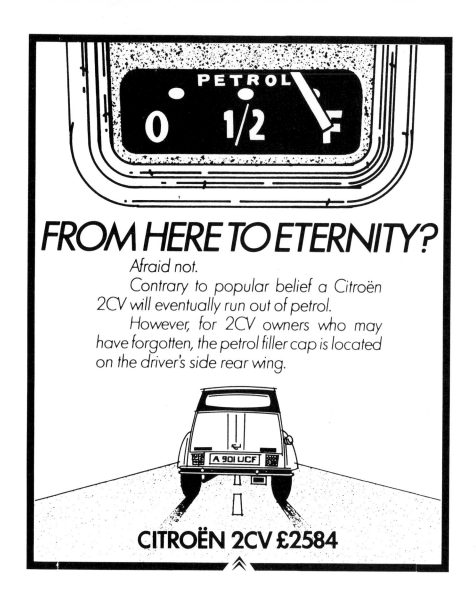

FROM HERE TO ETERNITY?

Afraid not.

Contrary to popular belief a Citroën 2CV will eventually run out of petrol.

However, for 2CV owners who may have forgotten, the petrol filler cap is located on the driver's side rear wing.

CITROËN 2CV £2584

Clever and off-beat, the UK advertising campaign, like the Dutch, made capital of sticking to the truth.

Above right: Dick Bruna's famous 'egg' sticker of 1973.

company – and the Stedelijk Museum simply accepted it as it stood. Citroën Nederland, however, had for years been making its own decisions in this area. The people who carried out these decisions included the copywriters and ideas men Hans Ferrée and Dimitri Frenkel Frank, names familiar from quite different creative activities and, most important, the graphics designer Karel Suyling, now a lecturer at the Arnhem Academy. Suyling became involved in the Citroën sphere of operations in a quite appropriate manner. He was the first-but-one owner of a 2CV in Haarlem, where he lived, and took part in the economy and handling trials conducted on the Zandvoort circuit. He won second prize (a reversing light, an unheard-of luxury on a 2CV at the time) and this brought him into conversation with Jean-Luc Froissart, then head of Citroën Nederland. He told Froissart that he was designing a car. The latter wanted to see this design but added: 'Don't think you'll ever get a contract from us'. A few months later Suyling

in fact received his first commission: to design a 2CV poster. However, when he submitted his design Froissart did not think much of it – the 2CV was depicted much too realistically. The artist should make it look lower and more streamlined than it actually was. Suyling refused to falsify reality. It took three weeks – but Citroën yielded before this honest stand. Thus the first Suyling poster appeared (quarto size, on rather nasty paper), followed by an endless series of his designs, all of them based on the fine, but so often despised, principle of truth in advertising. In this context it is amusing to record that Karel Suyling also had to do battle for weeks with this same obstinate director to be allowed to use the nickname Ugly Duckling, already accepted by the public, in company advertising! Suyling's great triumph, however, must have been the fact that his own limewood carving of a duckling mascot, in plastic reproduction, dangled behind the rear windows of countless 2CVs for years on end. Seldom has anyone proved himself right so graphically!

ANATOMY OF AN UGLY DUCKLING

Headlamps, adjustable from inside the car

Roll-back canvas hood for keeping your head cool

Windscreen washer

First-rate guarantee (on all parts)

Steering wheel lock, an effective protection against car thieves.

Brake fluid level – check light with test button

Three-point seat belts (advisable in all circumstances because of the high cruising speed)

Removable rear seat – useful for that day beside the river, for example

Generous luggage space

Adjustable front seal on rails

Air-cooled 602 cc engine of light metal, giving a cruising speed of 60 mph

Capacious petrol tank – holds 4¹/2 gallons or about 205 miles worth – in other words – based on 47 mpg at steady 56 mph

Independently sprung wheels and front-wheel drive for better roadholding

Standard radial tyres for a firm grip on the road

91

Rare Birds & One-offs

Whatever mad idea you have, 2CV owners will already have thought of something even madder. Owners of 'normal' cars do not readily pick up saws or welding irons and spoil the much-polished bodywork of their pride and joy. But Ugly Duckling owners have never seen anything objectionable in this. In the 1960s, before club membership and activities began to decline rather with the arrival of the 'me generation', there was one large 2CV club in Holland – there are now two smaller ones – which held an annual rally in Beusichem, a little place in the province of Gelderland; it was *the* occasion for proud DIY enthusiasts to show off their ingenious – or bizarre – handiwork. In 1968, for example, there was the man who had made a complete camper out of his 2CV. Do not be misled by the Swiss number plate in the picture: the ingenious fellow was of Dutch nationality. With a minimum of contrivance he raised the existing roof to standing height at the back, where he had installed the galley-cum-bathroom. Thus he and his passenger(s) – there are two berths – could do their cooking in the dry and without pains in the neck. The sink unit (or wash table) in the built-on boot was provided with hot and cold running water, a luxury that even the Rolls-Royce has to do without.

Talking of Rolls-Royces, there are quite a number of 2CVs going around with bonnets of that make. In England there is even a cross-country fanatic who tows his precious 2CV to events behind a Rolls: birds of a feather no doubt.

But let us return to the 2CV rallies: for the 1971 event the club magazine published a catalogue of all the adaptations, alterations, improvements and gadgets that were on show. Five closely printed pages were needed for a summary of thousands of hours of devoted tinkering. We will leave on one side such technical items as inspection lamps of all possible kinds, intermittent windscreen wipers and rear-window wipers and stereo radios, and list reclining chairs; attachable wind or sun screens; double floors for storing tools; hand

Opposite page: A pacifist's armoured 2CV – not a broken sword but a knot in the barrel.

Left: Dutch-Swiss 2CV with galley and bathroom to stand up in.

Below: Car belonging to the leader of the Waggelclub, one of the three 2CV clubs that have existed in the Netherlands. The biggest of them, Het Lelijk Eendje (The Ugly Duckling) had 12,000 members at its height. This club had its own magazine, edited by chairman Toon Smits, and no fewer than 168 editions appeared between July 1956 and December 1978.

throttles; sockets for electric shavers; enlarged petrol tanks; racing steering wheels; stainless-steel bumpers; luggage racks; a rack for cine camera tripod and tentpoles beneath the bonnet; luggage nets; window extenders; 2CV backpack; fitted alarms; cap on a chain for the tank; brass horns; toilet roll fittings; compasses; curtains; bicycle bells for use in town; rear flap for picnicking on; transistorized ignitions; Mercedes bonnet; tip-up beds, as in Dutch flats; tip-up chairs; windowseats; cupboards; roof insulation; ice cream bells; ornamental exhausts; draught-proofed doors; hygrometers for measuring humidity; extending roof rack with awning for shade; padlocks for the handbrake; hardwood bumpers; and chrome mudguards. And all these cutters, drillers and messers-about were consistent in announcing these fruits of their ingenuity as their 'own design'.

2CV with kitchen.

Two ways of making a camper of it.

Above right: Tyres and suspension make the 2CV recognizable in this racing guise.

In the Middle East 2CVs go around with their coachwork replaced by basketwork through which the air can circulate freely. In our part of the world the problem is rather how to keep the draught out. Whatever else the 2CV is, it certainly is not draughtproof.

Mindful of the fact that the Americans call the 2CV a 'blue jeans car', in 1977 the fashion editors of *Elsevier* decided to solve the draught problem by giving the vehicle some warm clothes. Margot Loumans was allotted the task and she cut out tight jeans to measure that fitted the 2CV as if it had sat in the bath in them. Even the headlamps were given studded denim covers. Side and back pockets were not omitted, nor were a leather belt and rivets in elegant patterns (*see* illustration, p.102).

Basketwork for ventilation in a hot country.

2CV with flower border and lawn behind, battering ram in front.

At Dronte in the Netherlands a Citroën agent and bird lover uses a 2CV in new, as yet trackless, polderland. He has mounted a muck spreader at the rear filled with maize grain so that he can feed the pheasants mechanically in bad weather.

Right: Brood of Ugly Ducklings on the water – the quickest way through Paris.

2CV with water pots – a mobile oasis.

Like ducklings to water

A duckling is in its element in the water – a thought that has occurred to many. Of course the 2CV is not an amphibious vehicle, although it can manage deep puddles and shallow streams with ease. However, 2CVs afloat are by no means exceptional. Some have taken the upper part of the bodywork and welded it on to steel fishing boat. They fish through the door, with the top open when it is sunny, closed when it rains, and the seats for support – this way even catching flounders can be a pleasure.

Others see more potential in the 2CV engine and use it to power their craft. Whether the 2CV-powered paddleboat constructed in 1971 by an 18-year-old student at the Amsterdam maritime school is still afloat is difficult to discover. If it just depends on the engine it will still be going in the next century.

A life of this length will not be granted to the bathtub 2CV in which two firemen competed in the races for these craft in Enkhuizen harbour in 1977. This was a normal production Ugly Duckling fitted with floats which crossed the finishing line without problems. And during a special celebratory week in the Dutch town of Sneek a 2CV mounted on barrels toured the waterways for the whole seven days, putting out its indicators when turning to port or starboard. It was the work of the local Citroën agent.

96

All hands on deck – crossing a river in India.

In southern Africa – the car is in the boat, but how do they get it out?

The motorship Gauloises I. *Note paddles on roof rack – a nice touch.*

97

One of the seven plagues?

2CV in Dutch national colours. Je maintiendrai (I survive) motto of the House of Orange, could also apply to the car.

Delivery van in pastel shades.

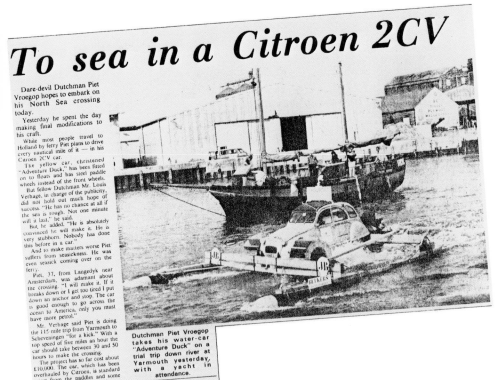

To sea in a Citroen 2CV

Dare-devil Dutchman Piet Vroegop hopes to embark on his North Sea crossing today.

Yesterday he spent the day making final modifications to his craft.

While most people travel to Holland by ferry Piet plans to drive every nautical mile of it — in his Citroen 2CV car.

The yellow car, christened "Adventure Duck," has been fitted on to floats and has steel paddle wheels instead of the front wheels.

But fellow Dutchman Mr. Louis Verhage, in charge of the publicity, did not hold out much hope of success. "He has no chance at all if the sea is rough. Not one minute will it last," he said.

But he added, "He is absolutely convinced he will make it. He is very stubborn. Nobody has done this before in a car."

And to make matters worse Piet suffers from seasickness. He was even seasick coming over on the ferry.

Piet, 37, from Langedyk near Amsterdam, was adamant about the crossing. "I will make it. If it breaks down or I get too tired I put down an anchor and stop. The car is good enough to go across the ocean to America, only you must have more petrol."

Mr. Verhage said Piet is doing the 115-mile trip from Yarmouth to Scheveningen "for a kick." With a top speed of five miles an hour the car should take between 30 and 50 hours to make the crossing.

The project has so far cost about £10,000. The car, which has been overhauled by Citroen, is standard apart from the paddles and some waterproofing, although it has a radar reflector and a radio. An outboard engine is fitted in case of emergency.

"We are following him in a boat just in case he goes down. He is wearing a survival suit so he will probably float for a few minutes," said Mr. Verhage.

● The record for amphibious travel was set up in the 1950s when Australian Frederick Carlin circumnavigated the world in a 24 ft. amphibious jeep. He arrived in England in August, 1951, after

Dutchman Piet Vroegop takes his water-car "Adventure Duck" on a trial trip down river at Yarmouth yesterday, with a yacht in attendance.

250 jobs lost

Two-thirds of the 380 workforce are to be made redundant at the giant Flixborough chemical plant, near Scunthorpe, which was rebuilt for £37 million after being destroyed by an explosion in 1974. The plant, Nyxro UK, was reopened in 1979 after the blast which cost 28 lives and destroyed homes in three nearby villages. The board of directors blamed the

Piet Vroegop never made it.

Economy best. In 1965 the president of the Norwegian 2CV club set an unequalled economy record in a mountain area. Using an ordinary production 2CV with 37,300 miles on the clock, and loaded with luggage plus one passenger, he made the journey from Oslo to Bergen at an average petrol consumption of 68 mpg. And he did not cheat by coasting downhill in neutral.

By far the most ambitious waterborne 2CV project was that of the Dutchman Piet Vroegop from Broek op Langedijk. In 1981 he planned to cross the North Sea from Great Yarmouth to Scheveningen in one. The car was placed on a 538 sq ft raft and this was carried on floats made from hollow tubes 15.75 in. in section with walls 0.9 in thick, which were packed with high-buoyancy material. Aluminium paddle blades were welded to the front wheel rims and these were driven by the ordinary 2CV engine. The enterprise, intended for inclusion in the *Guinness Book of Records,* did not proceed without problems and obstacles. The initial construction, with wooden paddle blades, and car inner tubes wrapped in sailcloth upon which to float, proved insufficiently seaworthy. It also proved necessary to have a separate handbrake for each of the front wheels, so as to be able to manoeuvre. Then during the trials on the North Sea off Egmond the police intervened. On 7 May 1985 the local station commander wrote to the enterprising gentleman under the heading 'Dangerous vessel/floating object at sea off Egmond aan Zee':

In accordance with the general police regulations applying in the district of Egmond, persons are prohibited from being on the sea or putting out thereto on air beds or air cushions, car tyres or any other such means of flotation (Art. 205 APV). Furthermore, in accordance with Art. 206 persons are prohibited from keeping on or introducing on to the beach any vessel not exclusively intended for the purpose of sea fishing. It is therefore my intention that if there is any repetition of this act proceedings in respect of infringement of these Articles will be initiated against you and any person or persons found on your means of flotation/vessel.

The letter appears more bureaucratic than it really was. Vroegop in fact had been rather slapdash in his preparations for the trip. It is true he had had some trials on the IJsselmeer, but he had absolutely no idea how the contraption would behave in a strong beam wind or high waves, nor what the petrol consumption would be on the 124 mile crossing.

At first he wanted to make his attempt on the Dutch national day, but his craft was not ready, and the weather was against him and the North Sea was a good deal rougher than he had experienced on the North Holland canal between Alkmaar and Kolhorn! However, by the beginning of July 1981 he was ready to start. The construction, named *Zee-eend* (Sea Duck) in the meantime, was shipped to Great Yarmouth. Sufficient sponsors were found for Vroegop to be able to pay for an accompanying boat with a skipper who had a thorough knowledge of the North Sea. Further trials were made – and in the end he did not set sail. The skipper of the accompanying vessel simply forbade the voyage when he saw how unseaworthy the raft became in waves that any little fishing boat would laugh at. His mission unaccomplished, Vroegop returned to the Netherlands a sadder and a wiser man. He and his 2CV, however, had had ample publicity:

Paddling Piet's 'Drive' over North Sea – To Sea in a Citroën 2CV – Strong Winds Delay Sailing Citroën as Deadline Near – Time and Tide Halt Sea Car – Duckling Can't Swim – Paddle-duckling Across the Sea – Flying Dutchman on Wheels – Piet's Double Dutch Drive – North Sea Crossing by Paddlewheel Car

We will bring this rather watery section to an end with the report that a few years ago, a French factory making polyester hulls put four water skis on the market with enough buoyancy to carry a 2CV across a river – without anyone getting a foot wet.

The 'back-to-back' 2CV is not as silly as it looks. Specially designed for the Provençal fire brigades, it enables a quick getaway when a team is confronted by fire on a narrow forest track.

Below: The barrel organ 2CV – but where's the collecting tin?

Bottom: Lengthened Pullman 2CV smoking room and bar.

Some odd specimens

In natural history terms 'duck' (with, of course, the diminutive duckling) is a name that covers an extensive family of birds whose members include the wigeons, the teals, Rouen ducks, Peking ducks, Bali, Campbell and tree ducks, the diving ducks and the pintails. In the course of its 35 years the automotive counterpart (*Anatidae citroënsis*) has increased by many strange species. Here are some of these *rarae avises*:

In Spain and the south of France there are 2CVs that consist of the front halves of two of the cars welded together. These were not 'born' deformed. These back-to-back 2CVs are for the forest fire-fighting services. It sometimes happens that in one of those tremendous forest fires that afflict southern Europe almost annually, a fire-prevention patrol is suddenly confronted by a wall of flame – and it is impossible to turn the vehicle round on the narrow forest track. The driver simply changes from one driving position to the other and 'hot-foots-it' off in the opposite direction.

In 1982 the French state cigarette company ran a promotion campaign in Germany for Gauloises – which are as French as the 2CV itself. For several months five remarkable examples of these cars drove around the larger German cities. There were: the no-parking-fines 2CV, provided with two fully fed parking meters welded to the rear mudguards; the Pullman 2CV with its body extended by 20 inches, with a smoking saloon and bar, table, Pullman seats and stereo; the floating 2CV with outboard motor; the street music 2CV with barrel organ on one side and the handle at the rear; and the graffiti 2CV with sides that could be written on (and washed clean).

In Naples there is a Dyane driving around whose engine packed up and that now serves as

Beatles 2CV: 'All you need is love'.

Opposite page, Top: Dutch designer Karel Suyling himself prepared these two textile pictures for use in an advertising campaign in women's magazines.

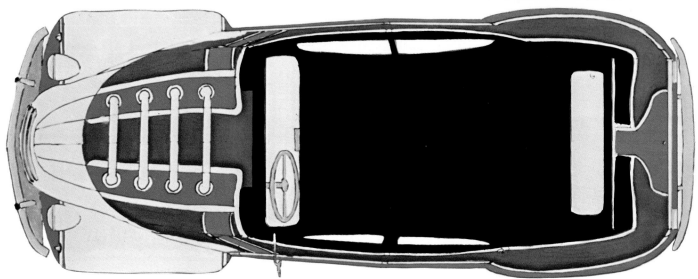

The 'Basketball Shoe' 2CV that composer Michel Legrand attempted to 'tame' in the circus ring during the Nuit des Etoiles.

Boot-hugging jeans for the 2CV from Elsevier's fashion editors.

And the 2CV ploughs on ...

Right: Un Cheval Vapeur?

Below: Air-cooled in front, ice-cooled at the back.

Right: Van + Van.

Bottom: Ice skiing.

a carriage for hire with a horse in front. An 'un cheval vapeur'?

Conversely, somewhere in North Brabant in the Netherlands there is a 2CV plodding over the arable pulling a plough. From 1 horsepower to 2.

A French ice cream man has extended his 2CV at the back to accommodate a chilled display counter from which he scoops out his wares.

Two members of the Rotterdam 2CV club have built a distinctive mini-caravan for their car. It is in fact the engineless twin brother – or sister – of the towing 2CV van.

An Amsterdammer, wanting to give his dog a view from the car, had the bright idea of fitting the 'porthole' from a washing machine into the boot lid of his 2CV. The dog now rides in the space behind the back seat, but can look out and see which car washes whiter than his master's choice.

There was an even bigger animal involvement on the part of the Englishman who, in the 1960s, used to take his donkey out for car rides. He just pulled back the roof, took out the back seat and installed the donkey. This was not to the liking of some asses of policemen, who took his (the driver's) name and address.

2CV on the slide

In the north of Sweden waterskiers have managed to turn their typically summer sport into an all-year-round activity with the aid of a 2CV. As soon as the lakes freeze over in the winter they exhange their speedboat for a four-wheel-drive 2CV Sahara. It reaches a speed of 37 mph on the ice without difficulty, with the 'ice skier' swishing along behind.

... and a 'winged' Duck

Among themselves 2CV owners try to outdo one another with their tall stories. Quite a few of them have been offered to the reader on the preceding pages. However, we have kept what is undoubtedly the tallest of them all in reserve: the story of a drive through the desert in *half* a 2CV. In July 1972 a team of four enterprising 24-year-olds set off from Grenoble for a journey of discovery through Africa.

They travelled in two Ugly Ducklings, both with more than 62,000 miles on the clock. Their destination was Cotonou, Benin's capital and port, via Algeria, the Sahara, Mali, the Republic of Niger, Dahomey, Togo, Ghana and Upper Volta. The journey passed without any problems until they suddenly found themselves in great difficulty on the way back, on the Mali-Algerian border: the chassis of one of the 2CVs, after too much punishment from rocks, potholes and other obstacles, as well as peppering by stones and gravel, gave up entirely. It broke across the middle, level with the foot pedals, and the engine block trailed along the ground. It would be impossible to cross the desert with this lame duckling; impossible, too, to continue with all the luggage in one car as has already been observed. However, 2 CV owners form a uniquely self-reliant tribe. In this case the gentlemen surgeons put their heads together and, after due consultation, decided on amputation. The engine was removed, the bodywork was sawn away ahead of the upright between the doors, dispensing with the windscreen, front doors, front seat, bonnet, mudguards and headlamps. The front suspension and wheels, with the supporting arms burned away, were bolted on to what was now the front of the shortened chassis. The broken-off front part of the chassis, which carried the engine, was pushed into the hollow supporting members of the rear chassis and welded into place: the four-seater saloon had become a two-seater sports coupé.

After this the shock absorbers, with the springs screwed down as far as possible, were attached to the steering gear by means of rings. To keep the vehicle in as horizontal position as possible the luggage was distributed strategically through the new 'filleted' 2CV, like the ballast in a ship. The engine threatened to subside and to keep it in place strong ropes were tied to the new front and secured to the roof above the doors. The half 2CV was ready to go: true it had no brakes, windscreen or wipers, and the petrol feed system consisted of a jerrycan at the front fixed directly on top of the engine – but such technical refinements are not greatly missed in the Sahara.

The operation took two days. After a good night's rest, doctors and patient were sufficiently recovered to proceed. In three days, the Sahara was crossed in the one and a half Ugly Ducklings without further problems.

How many half cars of any make have *you* seen driving around?

Across the Sahara by 'Fillet of Duckling'.

*Opposite: Thirsty ducks and
an Ugly Duckling.*

*Left: 2CV with
floral-patterned wallpaper.*

*Above: Camping in Norway –
a 2CV is not above drying
clothes.*

The 2CV as a sign of the times: the driver is looking for work as a graphics designer.

Below: Oil crisis 1973 – carless Sunday in the Netherlands. This solitary 2CV near the Coen tunnel, Amsterdam, has a German numberplate.

Last Words

And so we have come to the end of this account of the 2CV. Roaring, squeaking, sighing or groaning – but never failing – a whole procession of Ugly Ducklings has passed before us. Completeness has not been the aim. No doubt after reading this book many a 2CV enthusiast will remark that *his* story should have been in, that he knows of someone who went over Niagara in one, or went sponge fishing in the South Pacific. Writing, however, is a matter of gathering and sifting. A book such as this is too small in extent to allow everything to be said. Thus we have not dealt with the 2CV in motor sport, although the darned thing managed to come 12th in the general class in the 1959 Tulip Rally – when its top speed was still around 50 mph – in front of Peugeot 403s, Ford Fairlanes, Sunbeams, Mercedes 300SLs, Porches and Daimlers; and in class A it took the first two places. Cross-country in 2CVs has been mentioned only in passing (although of course this branch of the sport is more common in France than in regions further north).

Despite all the competition from other small or compact cars the 2CV, with its canvas top and a coffee grinder of an engine under its bonnet, has gone rolling on successfully for 35 years. Of course speed restrictions and increasing fuel costs have also played a part in its popularity. As far as these factors are concerned, the 2CV still has thing going its way. It would not be too far-fetched, therefore, to suggest that the makers will still be turning it out in 1998, when it is 50, and that it will witness the glories of the new century. Whether this will happen will depend on the makers, not on the drivers.

At a rally-cum-obstacle race for 2CVs organized in Holland in 1956 the participants had only to cover 43 miles in a given time. At the start, however, they learned they could only be counted as finishing the course if they were in possession of: a green acid drop, a fir cone on an oak twig, a ladder made from ten matches, an empty but intact eggshell ...

2CV-cross with elderly but much hotted-up cars. This sport is very popular in the south of Holland, Belgium, and especially France.

Last Words

Illustration Acknowledgements

The publishers wish to thank the persons, public bodies and organizations listed below for making available the illustrative material used in this book:

ANP: 85, 108 below
ANWB: 23
Avoine: 1, 26
Jack Arentsen: 82 left and right above, 92, 94 above left, left and right below
Beck: 36 above
Berserik: 66 above *Vanuit de 2CV* © Hermanus Berserik 1964, c/o Beeldrecht Amsterdam. Property of City of Utrecht; 66 below *Groot Drieluik met de klok* © Hermanus Berserik 1966-7, c/o Beeldrecht Amsterdam. Property of Arbeidsbeurs, City of Rotterdam.
J. Bokma: 75
Wim Boost: 37
Jacques Borgé and Nicolas Viasnoff (from *La 2CV)*: 8 left and right below, 12 below, 13 above, 20, 21, 22 above and below
Dick Bruna: 90 above right
César: 28, 29
Citroën UK Ltd: 31, 69, 90
Desclozeau: 27
Le Double Chevron: 5 below, 6, 7 above and below, 38-9, 42-3, 46-7, 49, 50 below left, 51, 54 below, 70, 74, 84 above right, 102 middle

Daniel Dufour: 36 below
Nicola Earwaker: 45 above
Eastern Daily Press, Norwich: 100
2CV Evolution Technique: 16 below, 17, 18
Michael Geilenkirchen, Heerlen: 83
Luc Hommes, Maastricht: 108 above
Wouter Jansen: 12 above, 56 below
Kerleroux: 50 below
A. Leenes: 3, 34 below, 67 above and below, 98-9, 102 below, 107 below
Henk van der Leest, Rotterdam: 44-5
Harry van Liempd, Veghel: 104 above left
Sabel & Daniëls, Amsterdam: 93 above
Karel Suyling: 90 above left, 103
La Terre en ronde, Paris: 109
Guy Teteau: 24-5
Tourpress, Assen: 73 above and below
Tout (journal): 69
Jaap Vegter: 89 (from *Wie doet me wat,* strip cartoons by Jaap Vegter, Uitgeverij Bert Bakker, Amsterdam, 1982)
Vettiko: 30 above
De Volkskrant: 9 below
Helmut Vonk, Rijswijk: 95 above
The remaining photos are from the archives of Citroën Nederland and Citroën France.